Welcome to the r12 student
Small Group Study & Devotional!

This six-week study and devotional is designed to help you explore what it means to be an r12 Christian – an authentic follower of Jesus Christ – with a group of friends.

During your time at home, you have five days of devotionals that will help prepare you to learn and apply the principles from Romans 12 before you attend small group each week.

Becoming an r12 Christian is NOT about religious activities or keeping religious rules… it is lived out in life's key relationships as we love God and love people. So the more important question becomes… how much are you becoming like Jesus? Being an r12 Christian flows out of a relationship with God. It's about experiencing His grace, not earning His love through performance. God is willing to go deeper to help you become like Jesus… are you ready?

TABLE OF CONTENTS

Today's Scripture
Philip ran over and heard the man reading from the prophet Isaiah. Philip asked, "Do you understand what you are reading?" The man replied, "How can I, unless someone instructs me?" And he urged Philip to come up into the carriage and sit with him.
Acts 8:30-31

Big Idea
God wants you to discover what true spirituality is all about.

Today's Thought
Are you ready for an adventure?

For the next few weeks, you're going to travel on a journey with your friends in your youth services and small group and on your own with this devotional as you discover what it means to be an r12 Christian — a person who lives out Romans 12. This week, we're focusing on an important question: What is true spirituality? In other words, what does it mean to be an authentic follower of Christ?

Today's verses come from a fascinating passage in the Bible. Philip encounters a guy from Ethiopia who was "reading aloud from the book of the prophet Isaiah," according to verse 28. This guy was searching for answers, and he recognized the power of God's written word to find those answers — but he needed help understanding exactly what Isaiah meant. It turns out that this Ethiopian man was reading a prophetic passage about Jesus!

A lot of people in our culture are searching for answers, too. They have this nagging sense that life holds a deeper meaning than just acquiring lots of stuff, impressing lots of people, and earning lots of money. Many people know that spirituality matters, but they don't quite know where to find it and how to experience it.

Maybe you're on a search. You're wondering what it means to become an r12 Christian. You want to know how your life can impact others. You have lots of questions, but you're not quite sure where you can find the answers.

Guess what? God's OK with our search for answers. God created humanity to think and reason and examine and seek and explore. Our questions don't scare God. (After all, He IS God!)

You'll discover what it means to be an authentic, growing, mature Christ-follower as you spend time digging into Romans 12 over the next few weeks. Write your questions in the blank space at the end of each day's devotional entry. Take your questions to your small group gatherings each week. Talk about these questions with your friends. And get ready for the adventure!

Prayer

God, I'm so glad You aren't afraid of my questions. I want to learn more about what it means to be an authentic, r12 Christian. Help me on this journey. I know that You hold the answers and that You'll reveal them as I read the Bible, spend time in prayer, and talk with my friends in the coming weeks. Thanks for the adventure You have in store for me. Amen.

Today's Scripture
Jesus told him, "I am the way, the truth, and the life. No one can come to the Father except through me."
John 14:6

Big Idea
Jesus is the best companion and guide for the road trip of life.

Today's Thought
Ever been on a crazy road trip? You know — the trip when your dad lost the keys to the rental car, or the trip when your friends KNEW that road was a shortcut, or the trip when your 20-year-old clunker decided it was time to die?

Oh yeah. Good times.

In many ways, life is like a crazy road trip. We have an ultimate destination, but the journey itself is where we have our greatest experiences. Our goal is eternity in Heaven with God, but how do we get there? Which path do we follow? Which roads do we avoid? How do we handle the roadblocks and obstacles and flat tires? How will we be changed by the adventure of being r12 Christians?

We can choose to navigate this journey on our own, but the wiser, better way is to turn to Jesus — almost like a spiritual GPS. (But maybe think of Jesus speaking with a more normal voice than most of those GPS devices use!) After all, Jesus told us that He's the way, the truth, and the life.

When Jesus said He is the way, it reminds us that He is the path. He guides and directs and leads us. When you feel lost, Jesus is the one who helps you get back on track.

When Jesus said He is the truth, it reminds us that He is the teacher. When you don't know how to handle a situation or what to say to a friend or how to apply something from the Bible, you can turn to Jesus for answers.

And when Jesus said He is the life, it reminds us that He is life's source and creator. Who understands the right road to travel any better than the creator?

If you're feeling a little lost or stuck or lonely today, turn to Jesus. He's right there with you — the best companion for the journey of life.

Prayer

God, thanks for giving me direction in this life. I know that I can try on my own, but I don't want to go through all the pain and heartache my choices could bring. I want my life to follow Your path because You have an incredible dream for me. Help me turn to Jesus for guidance and instruction and strength each day. Amen.

Today's Scripture

Then Jesus said, "Come to me, all of you who are weary and carry heavy burdens, and I will give you rest. Take my yoke upon you. Let me teach you, because I am humble and gentle at heart, and you will find rest for your souls."
Matthew 11:28-29

Big Idea

Being religious is tiring, but following Jesus is fulfilling, exciting, and satisfying.

Today's Thought

Pop quiz: You can tell when people have become mature Christians because they say the right words, do the right things, avoid the wrong people, wear the right clothes, and act nice to other people, right?

Answer: Not necessarily.

People talk about Christianity being a religion, and in a technical sense, they're right. But being a follower of Christ isn't the same thing as being a religious person — in fact, it's the opposite!

Religious people are convinced that God's love is directly related to their actions and deeds. They believe they can earn God's love and acceptance — or they think God will stop loving them if they don't act a certain way or perform well enough, as if God were a judge on American Idol. That's a recipe for burnout, fatigue, and disappointment because our human efforts will always fall short.

Look at what Jesus said in Matthew 11. He called out to people who were burned out on religion, tired of following routines and rituals, and exhausted by trying to earn God's love. Jesus promises a different life, one filled with rest, refreshment, and joy. That's the sign of true spirituality and an authentic, vibrant relationship with God.

God's love isn't based on your performance. You can't earn forgiveness. You can't work your way into Heaven. Forgiveness, salvation, eternal life, a fulfilling life on this earth — these things are experienced through a relationship with Jesus.

Ultimately, God is more concerned about what's happening inside of us than what we do on the outside — and if we're becoming more like Jesus on the inside, it's going to be obvious on the outside! Our lives will reflect that change. That's part of our experience as r12 Christians. Focus on your relationship with Jesus, and change will happen!

Prayer

God, help me to avoid the trap of performing religious duties just to please You. Help me experience and understand what it means to find rest, refreshment, and joy in my relationship with You. Thanks for loving me, even when I don't deserve it. Change and transform me into the person You want me to be — from the inside out. Amen.

Today's Scripture

Jesus replied, "'You must love the Lord your God with all your heart, all your soul, and all your mind.' This is the first and greatest commandment. A second is equally important: 'Love your neighbor as yourself.'"
Matthew 22:37-39

Big Idea

Love God and love other people — that's the heart of true spirituality.

Today's Thought

Who's your role model?

Thanks to our life experiences, most of us know that if we want to learn a new skill or sport or instrument, it's best to find a role model — someone who knows the ropes and can teach us the tricks of the trade. Watch this person closely. Imitate this person. Use this person as the model.

What about our journey to become r12 Christians? Who's the best role model?

True spirituality is defined and grown by loving God and loving other people. And in our journey to understand and experience true spirituality, our best role model is Jesus.

Jesus' words here in Matthew 22 are really insightful. Did you realize that these two commandments summarize the big themes of the Ten Commandments? Seriously! Take a look at Exodus 20 and you'll see that the first four commandments involve our relationship with God, and the final six commandments involve our relationship with other people. Jesus took an entire chapter and condensed it down to one text message — give or take a few characters.

And as you examine Jesus' life in the Gospels — Matthew, Mark, Luke, and John — you discover that He didn't just talk about loving God and loving others. He lived it out. Jesus loved His Father with every part of His life. Jesus regularly spent time praying to God the Father.

Jesus loved the outcasts and sinners and ordinary folks. He loved the people who followed Him and the people who rejected Him. Jesus loved the people who betrayed Him — even when it was one of His own disciples. Jesus' lifestyle matched His instructions. That's why Jesus is our perfect role model for true spirituality.

Prayer

God, You know that I want to love You and other people. And You know that some days I do pretty well, but other days I really struggle. Would you help me today? I want my life to reflect the life Jesus led, with a love for You and a love for the people around me. This isn't my natural attitude, so I'm depending on You to help me grow in this area. But I know it's Your desire for my life, so together we can make it through today. Amen.

Today's Scripture

For I am not ashamed of this Good News about Christ. It is the power of God at work, saving everyone who believes—the Jew first and also the Gentile. This Good News tells us how God makes us right in his sight. This is accomplished from start to finish by faith. As the Scriptures say, "It is through faith that a righteous person has life."
Romans 1:16-17

Big Idea

God is working in your life today, and He will be working in your life tomorrow.

Today's Thought

OK, time for a case of good news/bad news. Let's start with the bad news: You're human and you will never be perfect — even if you follow Jesus for 100 years. Sorry. Hate to be so blunt, but it's true.

So, what's the good news? Even the greatest Christians in history were imperfect — people like Billy Graham, the Apostle Paul, Mother Teresa, and Martin Luther. God was still working in their lives, helping them mature and become more like Jesus until the day they died.

Most of us wish we could just push a button and suddenly achieve Jesus-like status. But it's reassuring to realize that generations of Christ-followers have traveled this same journey of spiritual growth — the journey of growing closer to God.

Think back to the day you decided to follow Jesus. Maybe it was a week ago, or a year ago, or five years ago. How are you different today? How has God helped you with anger or lust or greed or impatience? What are some ways you're more like Jesus today than you were on that day you became a Christian? (And hey, if you haven't yet made the decision to follow Jesus but you want to know more, check out page 87 here in this devotional.)

Right now, pause and think of three ways you're different because of your relationship with Jesus. Write them down in the blank space at the end of today's devotional.

And then take time today to thank God for the ways you've changed during your spiritual journey. If it's a huge change, that's awesome! If it's a bunch of small, tiny changes, that's awesome too! Every change is a reminder that God has worked in your life and is continuing to work in your life — and an encouragement to keep trusting God to change and transform you as an r12 Christian.

Prayer

God, thanks for all the ways You've worked in my life and how You're helping me today to become a more authentic, committed follower of Jesus. On the days I get discouraged because I don't see the evidence of change in my life, remind me of the person I used to be and how I'm no longer that person. Thanks for Your love, forgiveness, and patience. Amen.

What is True Spirituality?

think about it

You're a teenager, which means you like to dream. You dream about the future. You dream about life's opportunities. You dream about places you'll visit and people you'll meet. You dream about your first job and first car and meeting the perfect spouse and buying a house and starting a family — it's an endless list for most teenagers.

God has dreams and desires for your life, too. Maybe you'd never thought of it before, but it's true. God wants you to love Him, to spend time with Him, to reflect His characteristics, to care for others, to become more like Jesus, and to authentically display your faith. That's God's dream — that you and I would live like r12 Christians.

get it started

The New Testament — especially the Gospels of Matthew, Mark, Luke, and John — talk a lot about Jesus and His disciples. What does the word "disciple" mean to you?

If you hear someone talking about "spiritual maturity," what does that phrase mean to you?

Pair up with another person in the group and take a couple of minutes to answer this question:
What are some signs or pieces of evidence you would see in the life of someone who is a spiritually mature follower of Jesus?

Come back together as a group to discuss your answers to the previous question.

For the next few weeks, our small group is embarking on an adventure to discover what it means to be r12 Christians. Think of it as a voyage into new terrain, an expedition on a spiritual journey God has planned for you. Romans 12 will be your guidebook — or roadmap, if you like that image.

Read Romans 12 as a group:

[1]"And so, dear brothers and sisters, I plead with you to give your bodies to God

because of all he has done for you. Let them be a living and holy sacrifice—the kind he will find acceptable. This is truly the way to worship him.

²Don't copy the behavior and customs of this world, but let God transform you into a new person by changing the way you think. Then you will learn to know God's will for you, which is good and pleasing and perfect.

³Because of the privilege and authority God has given me, I give each of you this warning: Don't think you are better than you really are. Be honest in your evaluation of yourselves, measuring yourselves by the faith God has given us. ⁴Just as our bodies have many parts and each part has a special function, ⁵so it is with Christ's body. We are many parts of one body, and we all belong to each other.

⁶In his grace, God has given us different gifts for doing certain things well. So if God has given you the ability to prophesy, speak out with as much faith as God has given you. ⁷If your gift is serving others, serve them well. If you are a teacher, teach well. ⁸If your gift is to encourage others, be encouraging. If it is giving, give generously. If God has given you leadership ability, take the responsibility seriously. And if you have a gift for showing kindness to others, do it gladly.

⁹Don't just pretend to love others. Really love them. Hate what is wrong. Hold tightly to what is good. ¹⁰Love each other with genuine affection, and take delight in honoring each other. ¹¹Never be lazy, but work hard and serve the Lord enthusiastically. ¹²Rejoice in our confident hope. Be patient in trouble, and keep on praying. ¹³When God's people are in need, be ready to help them. Always be eager to practice hospitality.

¹⁴Bless those who persecute you. Don't curse them; pray that God will bless them. ¹⁵Be happy with those who are happy, and weep with those who weep. ¹⁶Live in harmony with each other. Don't be too proud to enjoy the company of ordinary people. And don't think you know it all!

¹⁷Never pay back evil with more evil. Do things in such a way that everyone can see you are honorable. ¹⁸Do all that you can to live in peace with everyone.

¹⁹Dear friends, never take revenge. Leave that to the righteous anger of God. For the Scriptures say, "I will take revenge; I will pay them back," says the Lord.

²⁰Instead, "If your enemies are hungry, feed them. If they are thirsty, give them something to drink. In doing this, you will heap burning coals of shame on their heads."

²¹Don't let evil conquer you, but conquer evil by doing good."
Romans 12:1-21 (NLT)

This passage of Scripture provides an incredible summary of what it means to be an r12 Christian. And these verses help us understand five kinds of relationships we have in our lives. An r12 Christian is growing in all of these areas:

Your relationship with _____
     This grows when you are *Surrendered to God* (v. 1)

Your relationship with the _____
     This grows when you are *Separate from the world* (v. 2)

Your relationship with _____
     This grows when you are *Sober in self-assessment* (v. 3-8)

Your relationship with _____
     This grows when you are *Serving in love* (v. 9-13)

Your relationship to _____
     This grows when you are *Supernaturally responding to evil with good* (v. 14-21)

This kind of mature Christianity is relational. It's not performance driven, and it's not about religious rules and regulations.

Unfortunately, a lot of Christians seem to be heading in a different direction. We talk a good game, but aren't fulfilling God's dream for us. Some people call it "Consumer Christianity" or "Cultural Christianity" — in other words, what's in it for me? This breaks God's heart.

talk it over

How have your dreams about the future changed since you were a kid?

Do you spend more time thinking about WHAT you will do when you grow up or WHO you will become when you grow up? What's the difference between those two questions, and which do you think God wants you to do more?

What's the significance of being the KIND of person God desires?

What are some specific dreams you believe God has for your life?

Can you be a Christian without being an authentic follower of Jesus? Explain your answer.

Pair up with another person in the group for the next couple of questions:
What words would you use to describe your relationship with God right now?

How have you grown spiritually in the last few weeks?
How about in the last six months?
How about in the last year?

Come back together as a group for this final question:
What people have had the biggest impact on your spiritual life, and how did they play that role?

🌐 live it out

1. Read Romans 12 every day.

2. Read days 6-10 of your daily devotional.

3. Keep a prayer journal and write down your prayers, if you don't already do this; you'll be able to see how God is working in your life.

Today's Scripture

And so, dear brothers and sisters, I plead with you to give your bodies to God because of all he has done for you. Let them be a living and holy sacrifice—the kind he will find acceptable. This is truly the way to worship him.
Romans 12:1 (NLT)

Big Idea

Choosing to surrender everything to God is the beginning of an incredible r12 Christian life.

Today's Thought

You may already have your driver's license. If not, you're dreaming of the day when you'll be permitted to legally sit behind the wheel of your car, truck, SUV, or minivan and head out onto the road. Your parents have the same dream — but they might describe it as a nightmare.

But you won't get very far if you never put the key into the ignition and turn it. It's the first step in your driving journey.

How about your spiritual journey? Have you put the key into the ignition? Are you headed in the right direction?

Last week, you embarked on this journey with your friends in your small group and on your own with this devotional. The journey of exploring and understanding true spirituality will be much richer and more meaningful if you've made an important decision: **surrendering** everything to God.

The process of becoming an r12 Christian starts when we make the decision to follow Jesus and receive the gift of salvation. (Check out page 87, where we give you all the details on how to make that awesome decision!) But that's just the beginning. God is going to continue to work inside your life until — well, until the end of your life! We are all imperfect people who have the opportunity to become more like Jesus.

When we make the decision to become living sacrifices, as Paul talks about here in Romans 1, it's a commitment to surrendering everything to God and becoming an r12 Christian. We give God our lives, and we devote ourselves to honoring Him with every area of who we are: our choices, our hobbies, our friendships, our goals, our values, our ambitions, our dreams, our free time, and every other piece of our lives.

That sounds like a lot, right? But living for God this way is the start of an amazing life!

Prayer

God, thanks for how much You love me and desire the best for my life. Help me to surrender everything to You. It sounds pretty scary and intimidating, because I like being in total control of my life. But I know enough about You to know that you have even better plans for my life than I could imagine. Thanks for the work You are doing in my life. Amen.

surrender begins with an attitude

Today's Scripture

I once thought these things were valuable, but now I consider them worthless because of what Christ has done. Yes, everything else is worthless when compared with the infinite value of knowing Christ Jesus my Lord. For his sake I have discarded everything else, counting it all as garbage, so that I could gain Christ and become one with him. I no longer count on my own righteousness through obeying the law; rather, I become righteous through faith in Christ. For God's way of making us right with himself depends on faith. I want to know Christ and experience the mighty power that raised him from the dead. I want to suffer with him, sharing in his death, so that one way or another I will experience the resurrection from the dead!
Philippians 3:7-11 (NLT)

Big Idea

Your attitude opens the door to total surrender to God.

Today's Thought

Athletes know the truth of this simple statement: "Attitude is everything." If it's snowing on the football field, you still go out there with a winning attitude. If you're facing a team on the volleyball court that has won the state championship three straight years, you still go out and play hard as a team. If you're swimming for the first time since being sidelined by an injury, you still jump into the pool and compete with excellence.

Your attitude can make the difference.

This week of devotions is built on the idea of fully surrendering our lives to God. Paul displayed this kind of life, and you see his attitude in today's passage from Philippians 3. He knew what mattered in life — and what didn't matter. He discarded all the junk of this world and gave everything to God. That's surrender, backed up by the right attitude. Being surrendered means aligning our motives, plans, goals, and resources to achieve a specific task, accomplish a certain mission, or follow a particular person — in this case, God!

Having the right attitude toward surrender means wearing the right pair of sunglasses in life. Think of it this way: If you wear a pair with "negative" lenses, you'll see surrender as something to avoid because it's all about self-denial and martyrdom and giving up all fun. But if you choose "positive" lenses, you'll see that surrender is wisely recognizing that God has better plans and dreams for our lives than we do!

Sometimes we're afraid of surrender because we think it means life will be boring. But people who are totally committed to Jesus realize heaven is real, God is in control, God is calling the shots, God is good, and God will give us His very best when we do life His way.

God will accomplish incredible things in you and through you once you choose total surrender. It's part of God's strategy to make us like His Son… an r12 Christian.

Prayer
God, I need Your help with my attitude at times. It's so easy to think I'm the person that matters most in this world. Help me see things the way You see them. Help me discover more and more how much You love me and how You want the best for my life, and then help me to surrender everything to You. Amen.

surrender can be difficult

Today's Scripture

Then, calling the crowd to join his disciples, he said, "If any of you wants to be my follower, you must turn from your selfish ways, take up your cross, and follow me. If you try to hang on to your life, you will lose it. But if you give up your life for my sake and for the sake of the Good News, you will save it. And what do you benefit if you gain the whole world but lose your own soul? Is anything worth more than your soul?
Mark 8:34-37 (NLT)

Big Idea

God wants you to leave your selfish ways behind you.

Today's Thought

Me. Me. Me.

Did you realize that no one ever has to teach 2-year-olds how to say "me" or "mine"? It's just something every young child seems to automatically absorb, know, and understand. And we let them get away with it — to a degree — because they're, well, kids!

As we get older, we're supposed to learn how to share and get along with the people around us. But it doesn't always happen. We all enjoy being selfish. It's pretty easy to do, and our culture doesn't really discourage us from pursuing selfish dreams and desires.

God wants us as r12 Christians to experience a surrendered life, but it can be tough for us because it means sacrificing our spot as the most important person in our lives.

Surrender requires us to develop a lifestyle with God in first place. Surrender requires us to think about others instead of just focusing on our own needs. Surrender requires us to appreciate the gift of salvation we've received but willing to share that good news with others, too. Those are choices we make as we move forward with becoming mature followers of God.

And that's why surrender can be difficult.

Remember what Romans 12:1 said? Paul was talking about Christians becoming living sacrifices — total surrender to God. It would be easier to offer ourselves as *dead* sacrifices because we would no longer have any say! But being a *living* sacrifice means we have to continuously choose to surrender. It isn't a one-time event; it's a lifestyle.

Prayer
God, I want my life to be more about You and less about me. It's such a huge struggle, but I know it brings incredible rewards. Would You please help me today? I want to surrender the stuff that keeps me from becoming more like You. I need to focus more on You and others, and less on myself. I know that as I do this, You will continue to meet all my needs and provide and care for me in every way, and I thank You for that. Amen.

surrender is worth the cost

Today's Scripture
"The Kingdom of Heaven is like a treasure that a man discovered hidden in a field. In his excitement, he hid it again and sold everything he owned to get enough money to buy the field.

"Again, the Kingdom of Heaven is like a merchant on the lookout for choice pearls. When he discovered a pearl of great value, he sold everything he owned and bought it!
Matthew 13:44-46 (NLT)

Big Idea
When you consider the benefits of surrendering to God, it becomes an easier decision.

Today's Thought
Quickly — if you learned about a treasure that would turn you into a billionaire for the rest of your life, would you do everything possible to get your hands on it?

You probably answered yes — unless you thought you were being set up for failure, like a character in yet another *Pirates of the Caribbean* or *National Treasure* sequel.

God doesn't promise that He will make all of us billionaires, but He does promise to make our lives meaningful and blessed and significant as we become r12 Christians. And the promise of Heaven is a great treasure we can desire and pursue.

In these two brief parables from Jesus, we find people eager to sacrifice and surrender because they recognize the great reward that awaits them. One man found treasure in a field; he gladly sold all his stuff to buy the land and claim the treasure. The other guy finds an incredibly valuable pearl; he willingly auctioned off his possessions on eBay so he could purchase the gem.

These were easy sacrifices to make. Both men happily surrendered what they owned so they could attain life-changing treasures. Because these were parables, Jesus was attempting to teach his audience — and us — a deeper truth.

Jesus revealed that it's logical, smart, and wise to surrender everything to

God. And the heart of totally surrendering depends on our view of God — is He really good or not? Psalm 84:11 tells us that God withholds no good thing from people who are living right and following His ways. When we recognize how good and great and wonderful God is, we discover that surrendering is a reasonable sacrifice — just as Paul talks about it in Romans 12:1. Surrender truly is worth the cost.

Prayer
God, thanks for the truths You've placed in the Bible. Thanks for letting Jesus teach us through stories that help us understand You more clearly. I pray that You would help me pursue You and Your values and Heaven with greater passion in my life. Help me surrender all the stuff in my life, which ultimately doesn't matter. Help me to surrender my life, too. I want to serve and follow You with everything I have. Amen.

Today's Scripture

"The thief's purpose is to steal and kill and destroy. My purpose is to give them a rich and satisfying life."
John 10:10 (NLT)

Big Idea

God knows what He's doing when He asks you to surrender everything.

Today's Thought

Think of the most valuable, precious, important gift you've ever received. Picture it right now — or look at it, if it's in your room right now. One night you have a dream in which God tells you to sacrifice this valuable gift. He doesn't give you a whole lot of details.

Perhaps you could obey. After all, it's just a thing. It's just a possession. But what if God asked you to sacrifice a family member you deeply loved? Crazy thought!

When God told Abraham to sacrifice his son Isaac in Genesis 22, it was the ultimate test of faith. At the age of 75, Abraham had obeyed God and moved from his homeland to Canaan, part of what became Israel. About 10 years later, God told Abraham he would have a son and would become the father of a great nation. And about 15 years after that, Isaac was born — the fulfillment of God's promise.

Wow. That's a long time to wait! And now God tells Abraham to sacrifice Isaac? What was God thinking?

Surrendering everything to God means stepping back from the controls and giving up the driver's seat for your life. Is that risky? Sure! But you aren't surrendering your life to some random stranger or a person bent on your destruction. You're surrendering your life to the God who created the universe, who knows every detail of who you are, who loves you more passionately than anyone else in your life, and who wants you to spend eternity in His presence.

Abraham obeyed God. He was prepared to surrender and sacrifice Isaac. And at the last moment, God provided a ram to sacrifice instead. Abraham's faith and trust in God shone brilliantly in that moment.

As John 10:10 tells us, Jesus wants your life to be rich, satisfying, and meaningful — exactly the opposite of what Satan wants for you. Your life won't be the same once you surrender everything to God.

Prayer
God, I want to surrender everything in my life to You. I don't totally know what that means right now or how You might ask me to obey down the road, but I want You to be in charge of all that I am and all that I have. I want the rich, satisfying, meaningful life You've promised to give. Amen

Giving God What He Wants the Most

Surrender to God (Romans 12:1)

think about it

Want to stir things up and create a buzz among your friends? Change your relationship status on Facebook or MySpace. You'll get inundated with comments and text messages asking for all the details.

Beginning a friendship with God can create a buzz, too — but God wants to be more than just your friend. In fact, God's ideal "status relationship" with you would be summed up in this word: surrendered. It's one word that describes the kind of relationship God wants with each of us — our relationship with Him as r12 Christians. He's already sent you a request to change your status — are you willing to respond?

REVIEW

1. Last week's small group lesson focused on the "big picture" of being an r12 Christian. We saw how this one passage of Scripture examines our relationships with God, the world, ourselves, other Christians, and non-believers. Your challenges at the end of the lesson included reading Romans 12 every day this week and starting a prayer journal.

2. Your devotional readings this week focused on *surrendering* everything to God. You read about becoming a living sacrifice, having the right attitude toward surrender, leaving behind your selfish ways, recognizing the rewards of surrender, and preparing for a life that will never be the same.

get it started

Opening Question
Imagine being Facebook friends with God. What word would you choose to define your current relationship status with God? Why that word?

Interactive Opening
1. Why are the people in these newspaper and magazine articles considered successful?

2. Is their success lasting, or will it quickly fade away? Explain your opinion.

3. What are some of the ways our culture defines success — including success for teenagers? How much does the idea of *surrendering* fit into the cultural view of success?

4. How do you think these examples of success line up with God's perspective on success? Is this what God wants from your life?

5. How might God explain His definition of success? What role do you think surrendering plays in his definition?

talk it over

Read Romans 12:1 as a group:

"And so, dear brothers and sisters, I plead with you to give your bodies to God because of all he has done for you. Let them be a living and holy sacrifice—the kind he will find acceptable. This is truly the way to worship him."
Romans 12:1 (NLT)

This verse focuses on your relationship with God.

What do you think it means to be a "living and holy sacrifice"?

How can a surrendered life be a way to worship God?

Why does God want us to offer our lives as sacrifices? Why doesn't He simply force us to follow and obey Him?

What does it look like, specifically, to be surrendered to God?

What kinds of religious games do Christians sometimes play with their faith, with God, and with other Christians?

What's the difference between saying you're a Christian and living like one?

Read Matthew 13:44-46 as a group:

"The Kingdom of Heaven is like a treasure that a man discovered hidden in a field. In his excitement, he hid it again and sold everything he owned to get enough money to buy the field.
Again, the Kingdom of Heaven is like a merchant on the lookout for choice pearls. When he discovered a pearl of great value, he sold everything he owned and bought it!"
Matthew 13:44-46 (NLT)

Romans 12:1 describes surrendering as a reasonable sacrifice to God. In these parables, we read about two people who gave up everything so they could acquire something of greater value. Their friends might have thought they were foolish, but they were actually wise: They surrendered "second best" and received the "best of all."

Jesus used these two brief parables to teach a crowd of people about the importance of placing God's priorities first in our lives. God wants us to seek Him and His kingdom as the most valuable treasure we could pursue. What are some modern examples that would illustrate the same idea Jesus communicated?

Do you tend to think of "surrender" as being something negative or something positive? Why?

Read Psalm 84:11 as a group:

"For the Lord God is our sun and our shield. He gives us grace and glory. The Lord will withhold no good thing from those who do what is right."
Psalm 84:11 (NLT)

What does Psalm 84:11 tell you about God's character?

Pair up with another person in the group for these questions:
What areas of your life have you surrendered to God? How did you reach the place where you could make that decision?

What are some of the challenges you face in fully surrendering your life to God? How can we work together and hold each other accountable to grow in this area?

Surrender is the channel through which God's best and biggest blessings flow. God is waiting for us to go "all in" with our lives — total surrender to Him. That's the first step to experiencing God's greatness in your life. Are you all in? The answer is either yes or no.

live it out

1. Read Genesis 12, which was mentioned in Day 5 of your Student Devotional Guide. It's the story of how God called Abraham to make an incredible sacrifice in his life.

2. Read days 11-15 of your daily devotional.

3. Journal about the idea of going "all in" with your life. What does this mean to you as an r12 Christian? How can you do it? How can other people help you in this process?

Today's Scripture

Don't copy the behavior and customs of this world, but let God transform you into a new person by changing the way you think. Then you will learn to know God's will for you, which is good and pleasing and perfect.
Romans 12:2 (NLT)

Big Idea

You can choose to love the world's values, but choosing to love God is the better choice.

Today's Thought

What matters most in your life?

You may not spend much time thinking about that subject, but it's a life-shaping question. Your priorities guide your daily choices. Your values define the person you're becoming. Your goals shape your future.

Last week, we talked about surrendering everything to God. Once we make that decision, we're on the right track toward change and transformation in our lives. This week, we move into the next part of becoming an r12 Christian revealed in Romans 12: living a life that's **separate** from the world's values.

Notice that we aren't talking about living a life that's separate from the world — the life of a hermit or cave-dwelling monk. This isn't Yoda living on a planet away from the rest of all civilization. It's all about striking a balance of living IN this world without becoming consumed BY this world. That's why it's important to ask what matters most in our lives.

It's easy to copy our culture. It doesn't require much effort. Blindly watch all the TV you can. Visit any website you want. Hang out with friends regardless of their reputation or their impact on your decision-making patterns. Obsess over the newest gadgets and coolest fashions. Think about yourself all the time and ignore others. Turn a blind eye to injustices. Love the world.

God's plan is different: Love Him more than anyone or anything else. Instead of choosing to love the world and its systems of thinking and acting, choose to love God and His values, truths, priorities, and desires.

God wants to transform you into a new person as you change the way you think. It's the process of renewing your mind that opens the door to a growing love for God and a shrinking love for the world's values.

Prayer
God, You see all the pressures I face each day to love the world's values. It's so tough to focus my thoughts and efforts on loving You more, but I want that to happen in my life. Help me to pursue You and Your plans and Your priorities. Do Your transforming work. Amen.

you are what you eat

Today's Scripture
Think about the things of heaven, not the things of earth.
Colossians 3:2

Big Idea
Your daily habits and decisions help you become either spiritually healthy or spiritually weak.

Today's Thought
Ever heard of a guy named Daniel in the Bible? It's likely you know about the time he was thrown into a lions' den but didn't get eaten because God closed the lions' mouths. Pretty cool stuff. But there's another remarkable story that happened earlier in his life.

In Daniel 1, we read about how King Nebuchadnezzar of Babylon conquered Jerusalem and took Judah captive. The king ordered that the best and the brightest of the young men of Judah be brought to his palace for the opportunity to enter royal service.

We meet Daniel in this chapter when he convinces the king's staff to let him and three of his friends follow a different diet. Instead of eating the rich food and drinking the wine prepared in the royal kitchens, these four men wanted a different diet: vegetables and water. At the end of 10 days, these four guys looked healthier than all the other young men — and their diet became the diet for all the others, too!

You see, Daniel understood that if you want to be physically healthy, you need a healthy diet. Did you realize the same principle is true when it comes to spiritual maturity and health? It doesn't happen automatically. It happens as we pursue habits and disciplines and patterns that will help us become more like Jesus — a spiritually healthy diet.

As you move forward with this process of becoming an r12 Christian, fill your mind with stuff that draws you closer to God, not our culture. Spend more energy learning the Word than worrying about the world. Too many Christians — including Christian teenagers — are filling their minds with trivia and media and junk and celebrity gossip that pulls them away from God.

That's what it means to think about the things of heaven instead of the things of earth. Does this mean you should completely detach from your culture and become a monk? Not at all. It's not wrong to watch TV or read magazines or go online or play video games, but what do you see, how long do you view it, and what do you do with it once it's in your mind? Those questions matter as you go through the process of renewing your mind.

Prayer

I know there are so many voices in this world battling for my attention, God. Please help me develop a healthier spiritual diet. Let me feed on Your Word and Your truths. Let me hunger and thirst for a deeper relationship with You. Renew my mind and change my life. Amen.

Today's Scripture

The weapons we fight with are not the weapons of the world. On the contrary, they have divine power to demolish strongholds. We demolish arguments and every pretension that sets itself up against the knowledge of God, and we take captive every thought to make it obedient to Christ.
2 Corinthians 10:4-5 (NIV)

Big Idea

Satan will attack your life through the battlefield of your mind — but God is on your side.

Today's Thought

You may be a history buff. Or perhaps you struggle to stay awake in history class every day!

Maybe you find history more engaging when you watch those TV shows that tell the tales of World War II or the Civil War. They're great at helping us visualize the scene of the battle. Opposing forces fight over specific terrain. Generals plan calculated attacks around fortified defenses. The land is valued because of its natural resources or the access it provides to strategic ground. Capture a key stronghold, and you'll win the battle — or the war.

Spiritually speaking, your mind is the battlefield. The battle Paul describes in 2 Corinthians 10:4-5 is fought inside of you every day. It's a spiritual struggle that is waged in your mind.

The devil will employ every possible weapon in this battlefield. Doubt. Selfishness. Anger. Unforgiveness. Lust. Greed. Pride. Hatred. Bitterness. Dissension. Prejudice. Jealousy. He has an entire arsenal at his disposal.

But God's on your side. You aren't alone in this fight. God will help you demolish the enemy's lies. God will help you take thoughts captive and reject the ones filled with the enemy's venom.

That's why it's so important to realize how God sees you, how much God loves you, and who God created you to be. In Ephesians 6:17, Paul encourages us to "put on salvation as your helmet" as we prepare for spiritual warfare. When we have this knowledge of salvation, we find confidence knowing that God loves us, no matter what. Satan tries to use guilt and condemnation, but if you've asked God for forgiveness, you're a new creation in Him! You don't have to listen to the lies about shortcomings and weaknesses and disqualifications.

So the next time you feel the enemy's troops heading toward the battlefield of your mind, remind them that the war is already over — you can even say that aloud as a reminder that God is on your side! You're an r12 Christian who's been saved by God, and He will help you win the fight each day!

Prayer
God, I don't want to lose the war that Satan is waging for my life. I know that You are the source of salvation and strength, and I know that You're on my side every day. Give me victory today. Protect my mind from the enemy's attacks. You are greater. I know this and believe this. Amen.

Today's Scripture
Do not love this world nor the things it offers you, for when you love the world, you do not have the love of the Father in you. For the world offers only a craving for physical pleasure, a craving for everything we see, and pride in our achievements and possessions. These are not from the Father, but are from this world. And this world is fading away, along with everything that people crave. But anyone who does what pleases God will live forever.
1 John 2:15-17 (NLT)

Big Idea
You become stronger when you know where you are weakest.

Today's Thought
Sometimes we struggle to understand what a passage of the Bible is communicating. It can feel old, confusing, and weird — just like your math teacher! But you can understand 1 John 2:15-17 vividly by picking up a copy of almost any magazine targeting young people. These verses talk about three strategies Satan uses to drag us away from God's priorities.

Satan targets our passion to *feel* with a craving for physical satisfaction — lust of the flesh. It's a temptation to pursue pleasure. Satan targets our passion to *have* with a craving for things we see — lust of the eyes. It's a temptation to pursue possessions. And Satan targets our passion to *be* with a pride in our achievements and possessions — the pride of life. It's a temptation to pursue status.

But these aren't new temptations. Satan successfully used the same tricks with Adam and Eve back in Genesis 3 — and unsuccessfully tried the same approach against Jesus in Matthew 4.

What's your area of vulnerability? Maybe it's that good-looking classmate or the website you know you shouldn't visit. Maybe it's that dream of having a brand-new car or a wardrobe that always reflects the latest trends. Or perhaps you feel such a deep urge to be the most popular kid at school.

Your area of weakness is where Satan will attack you. Guaranteed. So, how can you prepare yourself for the battle that's ahead? Take 1 John 2:17 and make it your theme verse for the next few days. Write it down on a 3x5 card and tape it to your bathroom mirror or your car's dashboard or the refrigerator or a book — somewhere you'll see it several times each day. Memorize the verse.

Remind yourself that your goal as an r12 Christian is to live a life that pleases God, but Satan is trying to knock you off track!

Avoid the places and thoughts and people that make you more vulnerable. Renew your mind. Pray for God's help. Think about God-honoring things. Maybe even talk with a close friend who can hold you accountable in your area of greatest weakness. And most of all, remember that God is on your side!

Prayer

God, I know I'm an imperfect person. I have areas of weakness. I stand on Your Word and Your promises to be with me at all times. Guard my mind and my heart as I continue growing as an r12 Christian. Protect me where I'm weak, and give me Your strength today — and every day. Amen.

Today's Scripture
Study this Book of Instruction continually. Meditate on it day and night so you will be sure to obey everything written in it. Only then will you prosper and succeed in all you do.
Joshua 1:8 (NLT)

Big Idea
Spending time in the Bible is vital to God's process of transformation in your life.

Today's Thought
This week, we've talked about the importance of renewing our mind as we go through this process of becoming an r12 Christian. And some of you already have been asking, "Yeah, but *how* do I renew my mind?" Great question! Here are five tips.

1. Read God's Word
Spend time reading the Bible each day. Find your favorite quiet spot at home, grab something to drink, and see what God has written in His love letter to you. Don't approach Bible reading as a boring religious duty. Read with the expectation that God wants to speak to you through His living Word.

2. Hear God's Word
Sometimes it helps to hear the Bible being read by another person — maybe on CD or an MP3 file, or in a sermon at church. Or you could buy some music that is built on the words of Scripture. Our ears are powerful tools for absorbing knowledge and information.

3. Study God's Word
Learn about the Bible and how it was written. Use study tools online or from your local Christian bookstore. Get a Bible that has a study guide included.

4. Memorize God's Word
Choose one verse to memorize and start with it. Write it down on a note card and post it on your bathroom mirror. Build your mental database of what God says in the Bible and how God has used people in earlier generations. In many ways, this is one of the best tools for growing spiritually because it helps God's Word become a part of who you are.

5. Meditate on God's Word

This simply means to take a verse or idea from Scripture and think about it — ponder, meditate, chew on its meaning. You're bombarded with negative thinking all day. Spend a few minutes focused on a nugget of truth from the Bible!

Prayer

God, thanks for the Bible. Thank You for loving me so much that You gave me a book that talks about the great things You have done for the people who have followed You. Help me fall in love with You through Your Word. Give me a hunger for reading, hearing, studying, memorizing, and meditating on the Bible regularly and consistently. Amen.

Getting God's Very Best

Separate from the world's values (Romans 12:2)

think about it

It can be tough to live a healthy lifestyle in this country. We're busy, we have numerous responsibilities, and sometimes it's just so tough to say "no" to that super large soda, that extra-rich dessert, or that deep-dish pizza. But to remain healthy physically, we need to be aware of the consequences our nutritional habits have on our bodies.

If we aren't doing so well with our physical nutrition, it's likely we'll hear about it on our next visit to the doctor! But what about our "spiritual" diets? What does it mean to pursue spiritual health as an r12 Christian? And is it even possible living in this culture?

REVIEW

1. Last week's small group lesson focused on *surrendering* everything to God as r12 Christians. We talked about what it means to be a living sacrifice for God and how surrender is the channel through which God's best and biggest blessings flow. Your challenges at the end of the lesson included reading Genesis 12 and journaling about what it means to go "all in" as an r12 Christian.

2. Your devotional readings this week focused on being separate from the world's values. You read about choosing to love God instead of the world's ways, eating a "spiritually nutritious" diet, preparing for the battle in your mind, knowing your areas of weakness, and following five tips for renewing your mind.

get it started

<u>Opening Question</u>
Several verses in the Bible talk about "eating" God's truth or seeing God's Word as something we can consume (including Jeremiah 15:16, Ezekiel 3:1-3, and Revelation 10:9-10.) What do you think this idea means? How is it relevant to you today?

<u>Interactive Opening</u>
1. Where might you go if you wanted the tastiest meals, and why? What if you wanted the *healthiest* meals, and why?

2. At your age, you might not think much about the nutritional value of the food you eat. Why will this matter more as you get older?

3. What might be some similarities and parallels between physical food and spiritual food?

4. How spiritually healthy are you right now? If you don't know, how might you figure out an answer to that question?

talk it over

What do you think is the difference between making a decision to follow Jesus and then becoming a disciple of Jesus?

Read Romans 12:2 as a group:

"Don't copy the behavior and customs of this world, but let God transform you into a new person by changing the way you think. Then you will learn to know God's will for you, which is good and pleasing and perfect."
Romans 12:2 (NLT)

This verse focuses on your relationship with the world

Why do many Christians copy or imitate the behavior and patterns and choices of our world and culture? What are some consequences if we do this?

Why and how does changing the way you think contribute to God's work of transformation in your life?

Paul wrote that God's will for you is good and pleasing and perfect. What does each of those three words mean to you, and what emotions do they evoke?

What words would you use to describe the experience of choosing to go your own direction and ignoring God's will?

What does Romans 12:2 tell you about the process of change and spiritual growth? How much responsibility falls on God's shoulders and how much falls on your shoulders as an r12 Christian?

Last week, we talked about the importance of surrendering everything to God. How does this fit into the ideas of being separate from the world and renewing our minds?

If you've read the devotional guide this past week, you're already familiar with these five tips for renewing your mind as an r12 Christian:

_____ God's Word
"God blesses the one who reads the words of this prophecy to the church, and he blesses all who listen to its message and obey what it says, for the time is near."
Revelation 1:3 (NLT)

_____ God's Word
"Consequently, faith comes from hearing the message, and the message is heard through the word about Christ."
Romans 10:17 (TNIV)

_____ God's Word
"Work hard so you can present yourself to God and receive his approval. Be a good worker, one who does not need to be ashamed and who correctly explains the word of truth."
2 Timothy 2:15 (NLT)

_____ God's Word
"I have hidden your word in my heart, that I might not sin against you."
Psalm 119:11 (NLT)

_____ on God's Word
"Study this Book of Instruction continually. Meditate on it day and night so you will be sure to obey everything written in it. Only then will you prosper and succeed in all you do."
Joshua 1:8 (NLT)

Read 1 John 2:15-17 as a group:

"Do not love this world nor the things it offers you, for when you love the world, you do not have the love of the Father in you. For the world offers only a craving for physical pleasure, a craving for everything we see, and pride in our achievements and possessions. These are not from the Father, but are from this world. And this world is fading away, along with everything that people crave. But anyone who does what pleases God will live forever."
1 John 2:15-17 (NLT)

Verse 16 tells us about three passions Satan uses against us. They're actually God-given desires, but Satan's goal is to twist and distort them into passions that we pursue in the wrong way and with the wrong motives — and that displeases God:

Passion to _____ — lust of flesh

Passion to _____ — lust of eyes

Passion to _____ — pride of life

What are some specific ways Satan might go after teenagers with these three areas of temptation?

Pair up with another person in the group for this question:
You probably spend a lot of time thinking about the food you enjoy eating. How about spiritual food? What kinds of "food" would help you grow as an r12 Christian? How are you doing with your "spiritual nutritional habits" right now, and what are some specific steps you can take to grow in this area?

Come back together as a group to share some of your answers to the previous question.

🌐 live it out

1. Choose one of the five tips for renewing your mind we discussed in this lesson, and practice one of them every day this week. Journal about this experience, and see what God reveals to you and how He challenges you through this practice.

2. Read days 16-20 of your daily devotional.

3. Take a NO/YES challenge. Say "no" to something in your life — maybe take a media fast this week from Facebook or video games or your favorite TV shows. Say "yes" to using that time each day to read your Bible, pray, journal, listen to worship music, or reflect on God.

Today's Scripture

Because of the privilege and authority God has given me, I give each of you this warning: Don't think you are better than you really are. Be honest in your evaluation of yourselves, measuring yourselves by the faith God has given us. Just as our bodies have many parts and each part has a special function, so it is with Christ's body. We are many parts of one body, and we all belong to each other. In his grace, God has given us different gifts for doing certain things well. So if God has given you the ability to prophesy, speak out with as much faith as God has given you. If your gift is serving others, serve them well. If you are a teacher, teach well. If your gift is to encourage others, be encouraging. If it is giving, give generously. If God has given you leadership ability, take the responsibility seriously. And if you have a gift for showing kindness to others, do it gladly.
Romans 12:3-8 (NLT)

Big Idea

You have strengths and weaknesses — and that's exactly how God designed you to be.

Today's Thought

Years ago, one of the recurring characters on "Saturday Night Live" would regularly look into a mirror and utter these words: "I'm good enough, I'm smart enough, and doggone it, people like me." (Seriously, it was so long ago that your parents may have those words memorized — ask them!)

When you look in the mirror every morning — and yes, some of you look MANY more times during the day — you probably don't recite mantras to build up your self-esteem. But what do you see? What do you think about the person staring back at you? Are you proud? Embarrassed? Frustrated? Pleased? Unsure?

Most of us have mixed emotions when we look in the mirror. We see a person who has strengths and weaknesses. We wish all our weaknesses were strengths — and we wish we had other people's strengths! Let's use another word to describe this whole experience: Insecurity.

That's right. We battle insecurities. All of us do. Seriously!

Some folks cover their insecurities with bold, brash behavior. People keep their distance, and the real person remains hidden. Others cover their insecurities with quiet, timid withdrawal. People can't break through the walls, and the real person remains hidden.

But God calls us to have **sober**, honest evaluations of ourselves as r12 Christians. God wants us to recognize that we have weaknesses — and strengths. We can grow in our areas of strength and turn to others for help in our areas of weakness.

What would happen if you decided to embrace your weaknesses? How much deeper would your friendships become if you spoke honestly about your fears and failures?

Here's a challenge: This morning when you look in the mirror for the first — or fourth — time, remember that you are God's wonderful, marvelous creation! And if you feel the need to say that out loud, go for it!

Prayer

God, You know my struggles every time I look in the mirror. I want to be someone I'm not, and sometimes I wonder why You made me the way I am. Give me a better, sober, honest evaluation of myself. You are Creator of the universe, and You're the master designer of my life. Help me to see You working in me every time I look in the mirror. Amen.

Today's Scripture

You made all the delicate, inner parts of my body and knit me together in my mother's womb. Thank you for making me so wonderfully complex! Your workmanship is marvelous—how well I know it. You watched me as I was being formed in utter seclusion, as I was woven together in the dark of the womb. You saw me before I was born. Every day of my life was recorded in your book. Every moment was laid out before a single day had passed.
Psalm 139:13-16 (NLT)

Big Idea

Find your identity in God's incredible workmanship in your life.

Today's Thought

In case you haven't heard, God loves you. But we have even better news: God also *likes* you.

Sometimes we don't like the people we love. We're *supposed* to love our family members, so we do — but given the choice, we'll avoid Aunt Shannon and Uncle Will every chance we get because we don't really *like* them! (Maybe it's just the tacky homemade Christmas gifts we don't really like.)

God loves us. And *likes* us — even when we don't like ourselves.

Back in Exodus 3, Moses has a supernatural encounter with God at a burning bush. God called Moses to lead his people, the nation of Israel, out of captivity in Egypt. But Moses gave excuses. All he saw were his limitations. He didn't feel worthy of standing before Pharaoh. He didn't know what to say to the people of Israel. He wanted some ways to prove God had sent him. He claimed that he got tongue-tied too easily and wasn't very good with words. And finally he just said, "Lord, please! Send anyone else."

You get the sense that Moses didn't really like who he was! But when you read the words of Psalm 139, you discover that we *should* like who we are — unique and beautiful creations of God.

Many of us are held captive by shame — the same kind of shame Adam and Eve felt after they first sinned in Genesis 3. We live out of fear. We're afraid to fail, to be who we are, to be honest, to be vulnerable, to try something new, to risk making a mistake. It all goes back to the identity issue. God uniquely created you. You are eternally valuable, and you have the opportunity to continue growing as an r12 Christian.

And remember: God doesn't just love you. God likes you, too.

Prayer
God, thanks for loving me and for liking me. Thanks for making me so uniquely and wonderfully. I agree with what the Bible says: Your workmanship is marvelous. Help me to have a greater appreciation of Your work and my identity in You. I love You, God. Amen.

Today's Scripture
So now you Gentiles are no longer strangers and foreigners. You are citizens along with all of God's holy people. You are members of God's family.
Ephesians 2:19

Big Idea
Everyone wants and needs a place to belong in this world.

Today's Thought
God wants you to join a gang.

OK, those aren't quite the right words. But God knows that you're searching for a place to belong. It's part of the way you're wired. You want a place to belong — and you need it. You experience security when you have connection with others. You feel safer when you have friends who accept you and love you and value you.

That's why some teenagers turn to gangs. They don't feel secure at home, they don't belong to a group of friends who are headed in the right direction, and others have rejected them for one reason or another.

Back in Genesis 3, Adam and Eve suddenly felt insecure after eating the fruit God had told them to avoid. Their insecurity arose because they were vulnerable — they realized they were naked, and they felt ashamed. They were embarrassed by the "real" Adam and Eve.

Sometimes we're ashamed of the "real" us, too. We're convinced our friends would reject us if they knew our deepest secrets. We're certain our parents would be angry if they knew our darkest struggles. We want to be authentic followers of Christ, but we're ashamed of our imperfections — the evidence that we're "works in progress."

Today's Scripture comes from a letter the Apostle Paul wrote to Christians in the city of Ephesus, part of modern-day Turkey. When he uses the word "Gentiles," he basically meant anyone who wasn't Jewish — so pretty much, most of us! If you've decided to follow Jesus, then you're now part of God's family. You are unconditionally accepted.

And when you think about it, if you're part of God's family, why would you ever need to join a gang to find that sense of acceptance and security?

Prayer

God, thanks for loving me and caring about me, even when I wasn't following You. Thanks for loving me so much that You sent Jesus to restore my relationship with You. Thanks for making me part of the family. Today, give me an opportunity to reach out to someone else and help that person belong and feel more secure. Amen.

Today's Scripture
For we are God's masterpiece. He has created us anew in Christ Jesus, so we can do the good things he planned for us long ago.
Ephesians 2:10 (NLT)

Big Idea
You will find fulfillment and satisfaction as you serve God and others in the local church.

Today's Thought
Last time we checked, no one likes to feel insignificant, overlooked, or ignored. In fact, it's a huge bummer when we feel that way! Everyone likes being valued and appreciated. The search for significance is part of the human experience, but too often we search in the wrong places.

We find a measure of our self-worth through the things we do: our hobbies, our career, our activities, and our pastimes. What we *do* matters. That's how God wired us.

The Bible reveals God's plan for helping us find significance: using our talents, skills, resources, and spiritual gifts to serve others. We're told that whatever we can do, to do it well.

Get focused on what you were made to do, because this is who you are, the church is where you belong, and this is your responsibility. What's your primary spiritual gift? What's your collection of gifts and skills and passions around it?

If you don't already know, talk with your youth pastor or another leader about finding the answers. True significance as an r12 Christian is found in a selfless use of these gifts, and you will experience incredible moments of joy as you serve God and others in the local church.

You're a child of God. You belong to the body of Christ. You have the opportunity to discover, develop, and deploy your spiritual gifts. God gifted you to fulfill his purpose. You are uniquely significant.

We dare you to dream the biggest, craziest, most amazing dreams for how you can lead a significant, meaningful life — because God can dream even bigger, crazier, and more amazing dreams for you!

Prayer

God, thanks for making me the way You did. Thanks for the talents and skills and spiritual gifts You've given me. Give me opportunities to discover, develop, and deploy these gifts for your glory and honor. Don't let it be about me. Let it be about serving You and serving others as an r12 Christian. Amen.

Today's Scripture
Obviously, I'm not trying to win the approval of people, but of God. If pleasing people were my goal, I would not be Christ's servant.
Galatians 1:10 (NLT)

Big Idea
Live a life that pleases God, and you will discover your true identity, security, and significance.

Today's Thought
Are you a people-pleaser?

We aren't talking about a healthy desire to have peaceful friendships with other people. We're talking about an unhealthy obsession to make choices and live certain ways to make other people like us more. Yes, it matters what other people think about us — but we don't have to become captive to other people's opinions.

As Paul tells us in Galatians 1:10, God's approval is much more powerful than other people's approval. Some of us are so easily tempted to build our lives on the opinions of others. We wear what they wear, we shop where they shop, we talk like they talk, and we think like they think.

That isn't the ticket to becoming a world-class you. It's the recipe for becoming a top-notch imitation.

By the way: It's important to note that in this verse, Paul is NOT saying we can do anything to make God love us more than He already does. Paul is simply reminding us that from an eternal perspective, our relationship with God is what matters most.

If you build your life around trying to win approval or meet impossible expectations or attempting to earn God's love, then you won't be a "world-class you." It won't happen.

A "world-class you" is built on your commitments to knowing God, developing a lifestyle that points people to God, serving others in love, receiving and sharing forgiveness, absorbing and obeying the truths of the Bible and worshiping God in every area of life.

After all, the most attractive person in the world is the real you!

Prayer

God, I want to live a life that's pleasing to You. When I feel drawn to certain choices or lifestyles or patterns because I'm trying to impress other people, help me change course and refocus on You. I know that I can't earn Your love or forgiveness, but I want to honor You through my lifestyle, attitude, and interactions with other people. Amen.

Coming to Grips with the Real You

Sober in self-assessment (Romans 12:3-8)

think about it

OK, let's be honest: If you spend all day walking around and talking to yourself out loud, you will get some odd stares from people. It just isn't considered right. But every day, you have conversations in your head — self-talk about how you see yourself, how others might be seeing you at that moment, if your breath smells OK, if you're going to see that person you have the biggest crush on, and if your hair looks just right.

Sometimes we're too critical about ourselves. And sometimes we think too highly about who we really are. God says we need to walk the middle road: Recognize and appreciate strengths and weaknesses, and pursue a path that honors the unique way God has created each of us. God wants us to think humbly about ourselves. In other words, as an r12 Christian, you're called to not think too highly or too lowly of yourself — to simply not focus on yourself but to think of God and others.

REVIEW

1. Last week's small group lesson focused on being *separate* from the world's values as r12 Christians. We talked about ways Satan will attack our thoughts, and we discussed five strategies for renewing the mind: reading, hearing, studying, memorizing, and meditating on God's Word. Your challenges at the end of the lesson included practicing one of those five strategies during the week and taking a NO/YES challenge — fasting from an activity to spend more time with God.

2. Your devotional readings this week focused on having a *sober* and honest evaluation of yourself. You read about recognizing that God gave you strengths and weaknesses, finding your true identity, experiencing true security, discovering true significance, and becoming a world-class you.

get it started

Opening Question
What is a career or achievement or award that you'd like to accomplish or reach, but you know it probably won't happen because you simply aren't created or wired in the right way?

53

1. Why do some people fall victim to counterfeit money?

2. How can you know the difference between real money and counterfeit money?

3. What are some genuine things that the devil tries to counterfeit? Why does he choose those things?

4. How can you protect yourself from spiritually counterfeit things?

talk it over

What kind of "self talk" do you have most days? What are some ways your "self talk" guide your choices, actions, and attitudes throughout the day?

Read Romans 12:3-8 as a group:

"Because of the privilege and authority God has given me, I give each of you this warning: Don't think you are better than you really are. Be honest in your evaluation of yourselves, measuring yourselves by the faith God has given us. Just as our bodies have many parts and each part has a special function, so it is with Christ's body. We are many parts of one body, and we all belong to each other. In his grace, God has given us different gifts for doing certain things well. So if God has given you the ability to prophesy, speak out with as much faith as God has given you. If your gift is serving others, serve them well. If you are a teacher, teach well. If your gift is to encourage others, be encouraging. If it is giving, give generously. If God has given you leadership ability, take the responsibility seriously. And if you have a gift for showing kindness to others, do it gladly."
Romans 12:3-8 (NLT)

This passage focuses on your relationship with yourself

Verse 3 says that as r12 Christians, we need to have an "honest" evaluation of ourselves; other translations of the Bible use the word "sober." What's one area of your life where you've thought you were better than you really were? And what's an area where you didn't think of yourself as being as talented as you really were?

How do you handle this balancing act — recognizing your weaknesses and your strengths without becoming negative OR filled with pride?

What does it mean that all Christians "belong to each other," as Paul says in verse 5?

How would you summarize Paul's main point in verses 6 through 8?

Why do you think Paul decided to highlight these specific spiritual gifts?

Why are we happier talking to other people about our strengths but not our weaknesses — yet when we're alone, we sometimes become obsessed with those weaknesses?

What's so difficult about letting down our guard and revealing the real person inside? What are the risks, and what are the possible rewards? Let's talk about this for a few minutes.

We sometimes compensate for areas where we feel _____

and _____.

We all ask ourselves three central questions in life:

1. Who am I? It's about our _____.

2. Where do I belong? It's about our _____.

3. What am I supposed to do? It's about our _____.

Only God can provide authentic answers to those questions. Satan will attempt to deceive you into believing counterfeit things about yourself and seeking counterfeit solutions. This goes all the way back to the first book of the Bible and humanity's first sin.

Read Genesis 3:8-13 as a group:

"When the cool evening breezes were blowing, the man and his wife heard the Lord God walking about in the garden. So they hid from the Lord God among the trees. Then the Lord God called to the man, 'Where are you?'
He replied, 'I heard you walking in the garden, so I hid. I was afraid because I was naked.'
'Who told you that you were naked?' the Lord God asked. 'Have you eaten from the tree whose fruit I commanded you not to eat?'
The man replied, 'It was the woman you gave me who gave me the fruit, and I ate it.'
Then the Lord God asked the woman, "What have you done?"
'The serpent deceived me,' she replied. 'That's why I ate it.'"
Genesis 3:8-13 (NLT)

Three obstacles to getting the right answer:

1. We fear because of shame
How can shame create fear?

2. We hide because of insecurity
Why do our insecurities cause us to hide?

3. We blame because of denial
Why do we blame other people or life's circumstances instead of taking responsibility?

Three ways to overcome these obstacles so we can answer the three big questions:

1. Know who you are
God wants you to think accurately of yourself. This kind of thinking will free you.

2. Connect with other Christians
You were designed as one piece to a much larger body — the body of Christ.

3. Use your talents and gifts to serve God and others
Get focused on how you can use your spiritual gifts to honor God and serve others.

live it out

1. Read 1 Corinthians 12:4-11 and Ephesians 4:11-16. These passages of Scripture also talk about the spiritual gifts God gives His followers.

2. Read days 21-25 of your daily devotional.

3. Do a self-assessment this week. Take a 3x5 card, and draw a horizontal line in the middle. On the top, write "My Top 3 Strengths" and on the bottom, write "My Top 3 Weaknesses." Talk to your parents and your friends about who you really are — with the goal of reaching an honest, sober self-assessment. Bring the card back next week so we can talk about it as a group.

Today's Scripture
Don't just pretend to love others. Really love them. Hate what is wrong. Hold tightly to what is good. Love each other with genuine affection, and take delight in honoring each other. Never be lazy, but work hard and serve the Lord enthusiastically. Rejoice in our confident hope. Be patient in trouble, and keep on praying. When God's people are in need, be ready to help them. Always be eager to practice hospitality.
Romans 12:9-13 (NLT)

Big Idea
Authenticity fuels deep, meaningful relationships with other followers of Christ.

Today's Thought
Stop playing games.

No, not board games or video games or sports. Stop playing spiritual games. It's time to grow up and get serious about being an r12 Christian.

That message can be heard in Paul's words here in Romans 12:9-13, where you see several reminders of the value of authenticity and honesty. Don't pretend. Love genuinely. Be ready to help and eager to host — people who are **serving** in love.

God doesn't want Christians to play religious games. God doesn't want us to wear "masks" or create an image of who we'd like to be, instead of who we truly are.

Stop for a moment and think about the last time you walked through the doors of your church. Did you feel like you could really be yourself? Or did you feel the pressure to conform? Did you feel safe enough to talk honestly about your pain and your joy? Or did you find yourself using Christian jargon that made you sound holy and spiritual?

The church is designed to be a place of honesty and vulnerability — not spiritual games.

And God calls you to connect with other Christians as you serve and love and experience life together. You do it for the right reason and in the right way. When you begin to have those kinds of relationships, people will watch your life and see the reality of following Jesus. People will discover that God is real and sent Jesus to the world, and that's a more powerful message than any sermon can deliver!

Put away the games. Bring out the real you.

Prayer

God, I don't want to play spiritual games. I want to experience real, authentic, legit, true spirituality. Give me the boldness to take that first step of honesty and vulnerability with my friends, and help me do my part to build Your church the way You want it to be built. Help me to be the person You created me to be. Amen.

Today's Scripture
Don't let anyone think less of you because you are young. Be an example to all believers in what you say, in the way you live, in your love, your faith, and your purity.
1 Timothy 4:12 (NLT)

Big Idea
Don't sit on the sidelines — make a difference in your world today.

Today's Thought
This has to be one of the coolest verses in the Bible. Sometimes it feels like it's also one of the most overlooked, doesn't it?

Our churches are often guilty of telling you — sometimes overtly but usually subtly — that you don't become a "real" Christian or "real" leader until you're an adult. We talk about how kids and teenagers are the church of the future — and forget how insulting that can sound to you! You're the church of *today*, not just the future!

Some people think you can have less of an impact because you're young. It just isn't true. In many ways, you can have *more* of an impact because you're young! Way too many adults have been fooled into thinking they can't make a difference. They've become cynical and discouraged. But you're young enough to believe that with God, all things really are possible! (Pretty sure that's in the Bible at least once or twice!)

Timothy was a young leader in the early church. We don't know exactly how young he was, but Paul talks about his "youth" in several places in his two letters to Timothy. Look at what Paul wrote to Timothy in today's verse, and imagine if you got similar advice from a well-known church leader you respect. This leader basically says: "You know what? You can make a difference through your words, your lifestyle, your demonstration of love, your deep, growing faith, and your commitment to purity." You can be an example to other teenagers! You can be an example to younger kids! You can even be an example to adults!

With God's help, you can make a difference as an r12 Christian. You and your friends can make a difference. You and your friends and your small group can make a difference. You and your friends and your small group and your youth group can make a difference. (Catch the drift?)

Don't sit on the sidelines and let others impact their world. Get involved. Serve others. Meet real needs in others people's lives!

Prayer

God, I want to make a difference for You in this world. Let me see some real needs in the next few days that I can help meet. Use my friends and me for Your glory. Use our efforts to point people to You and Your love for everyone. Amen.

love people the way Jesus loved people

Today's Scripture
Jesus saw the huge crowd as he stepped from the boat, and he had compassion on them because they were like sheep without a shepherd. So he began teaching them many things.
Mark 6:34 (NLT)

Big Idea
Be like Jesus by filling your heart with compassion for other people — and responding in love.

Today's Thought
Don't you just love those Bible verses that compare people to sheep? Doesn't it make you feel like you should move out from your parents' house and set up a bedroom in a barn?

OK. Maybe not.

Set aside the sheep imagery for a moment, and look at a couple of profound things this verse tells us about Jesus.

First, during His time here on earth, Jesus felt human emotions — especially love. Jesus was God in human form. He was 100 percent God and 100 percent human. When His friend Lazarus died, Jesus wept. (He also raised Lazarus from the dead — the next time you attend a funeral, imagine how people would respond if *that* happened!)

Having compassion is different from feeling pity on someone. Compassion is rooted in love and grace and mercy. Pity is rooted in pride and arrogance and judgment.

At least one translation of this verse says Jesus "felt sorry" for them, but that really doesn't capture the right tone of His emotion. The Message version of the Bible says "his heart broke," and that's a clearer idea. Jesus had compassion on people in need.

But don't miss the second message in this verse. Yes, Jesus felt compassion. But He also acted! He did something in response. Your love for others will be displayed through your actions.

God wants you to experience compassionate love toward people who haven't chosen to follow Jesus yet — but God also wants you to act when you see opportunities to meet real needs in people's lives. That's the way Jesus loved people, and it's the way we as r12 Christians can love people, too!

Prayer
God, give me Your compassion toward the people in my world. Give me your eyes so I can see them the way You see them. Fill me with love and compassion and mercy, and help me share your good news with people who need salvation and a relationship with You. Amen.

Today's Scripture
"So now I am giving you a new commandment: Love each other. Just as I have loved you, you should love each other. Your love for one another will prove to the world that you are my disciples."
John 13:34-35 (NLT)

Big Idea
Don't settle for weak, insignificant friendships at church — go for depth and quality.

Today's Thought
Here's a fun experiment: Find a whole bunch of non-Christians and ask them what they think about Christians and churches. Depending on their honesty, you might be surprised and heartbroken at their answers.

Far too often, the world looks at Christians and sees people whose words and actions are inconsistent. You can help change this perspective: The more you show love to other Christians, the more non-Christians will discover it's possible to have an authentic faith in God. That's part of the experience as an r12 Christian.

The friendship between David and Jonathan offers a great model for the kind of love Jesus talked about in John 13. Jonathan was the son of King Saul and heir to the throne of Israel. David was a shepherd chosen and anointed by God to be, well, the future king of Israel. And somehow these guys were friends!

The Bible records some profound words in 1 Samuel 20:17. "And Jonathan made David reaffirm his vow of friendship again, for Jonathan loved David as he loved himself." What a strong bond of friendship! (If you have time, read the whole chapter of 1 Samuel 20 to get a deeper view of this remarkable friendship.)

Authentic relationships demand time, sacrifice, and devotion. Do it not just when it's convenient or on the way home. Show up. Go. Listen. Cry with them. Be part of the action sometimes. You know when you're genuinely loved.

That's how you can develop deep, quality, significant friendships at church. Experience life together. Love each other. Demonstrate your love through action.

The world will see — and take notice.

Prayer

God, I don't want to settle for weak, insignificant friendships with other Christians. I want to experience authentic community when I spend time with Your other followers. Let our love for each other become visible evidence of Your love for all of humanity. Help me and other Christians love each other in ways that honor You. Amen.

Today's Scripture
Since God chose you to be the holy people he loves, you must clothe yourselves with tenderhearted mercy, kindness, humility, gentleness, and patience. Make allowance for each other's faults, and forgive anyone who offends you. Remember, the Lord forgave you, so you must forgive others. Above all, clothe yourselves with love, which binds us all together in perfect harmony. And let the peace that comes from Christ rule in your hearts. For as members of one body you are called to live in peace. And always be thankful.
Colossians 3:12-15 (NLT)

Big Idea
Do your part in building deep, meaningful relationships with other followers of Christ.

Today's Thought
Let's jump right into today's passage of Scripture. Paul offers us four awesome ideas for building authentic community as r12 Christians:

1. Make a fashion statement for God
OK, it's unlikely you'll ever see a line of fashion called JesusWear, but God does care about your "clothing." Every morning, you *choose* what clothes to wear. It's a decision — and yes, for some of you, it's a long, painstaking, detailed process! But you have the freedom to choose. And God says you have similar freedom in how you clothe your life. You can be a jerk, if you want. But you also can decide to be merciful, kind, humble, gentle, and patient. Model some Jesus-style fashion this week.

2. Let the past be the past
Did you see what Paul wrote in verse 13? He said Christians should "make allowance for each other's faults." In other words, get ready to discover and experience other people's faults and shortcomings! Don't expect others to be perfect, because it just ain't gonna happen! (Apologies to all you grammar-loving teens.) And remember, you aren't perfect, either. Get in the habit of offering forgiveness — and receiving it when you mess up!

3. Be peace-seeking people
We can't always get along with everyone. But we can try, right? We experience peace from God as we pursue His plans for our life, and we experience peace with other people as we love them, pray for them, forgive them, and go through life together with them. Look for ways to resolve conflict, and search

for points of common interest with other Christians.

4. Be thankful
The more thankful we are, the more we appreciate the people around us. Be thankful for the friends who show up during difficult times in life. Be thankful for the friends who appreciate your jokes. Be thankful for the parents and grandparents at your church who value teenagers. Be thankful for all the skills, abilities, gifts, and interests God has given you. It's impossible to be too grateful or thankful.

Prayer
God, I want to experience real, authentic, genuine community with other people who love You and follow You as r12 Christians. Help me do my part to build these kinds of relationships. I pray that my church would be a place known as a place filled with forgiveness, love, compassion, and peace — and a place where Jesus' fashion is on display for a world in need. Amen.

Experiencing Authentic Community

Serving in love (Romans 12:9-13)

think about it

Nobody likes a fake. And plastic smiles don't last long when the heat gets turned up. True friends stand by our side during the best of times and the toughest of days. They don't abandon us, they don't walk away, and they don't reject us when they see our flaws.

We live in a culture that talks about BFFs, yet we see so many adults who lack deep, meaningful friendships with the people around them. Can you strive for something greater? Can you achieve solid relationships with others? Can you experience the kind of authentic community God desires for you? Yes, you can!

REVIEW

1. Last week's small group lesson focused on having a *sober* and honest evaluation of yourself as an r12 Christian. We talked about our search for identity, security, and significance, and how God offers the authentic answers — Satan only offers counterfeits. Your challenges at the end of the lesson included reading 1 Corinthians 12:4-11 and Ephesians 4:11-16, and doing a self-assessment with help from friends and family members.

2. Your devotional readings this week focused on *serving* others in love. You read about being real and authentic, meeting people's needs, loving people the way Jesus loved people, seeking quality friendships with other Christians, and building authentic community.

get it started

Opening Question
How long can you really stay friends with a person who always seems fake? How does that "fakeness" hurt your friendship?

Interactive Opening
1. What message does a gift of artificial flowers communicate?

2. Maybe you can't afford a dozen roses, so what are some other good, healthy ways to express your love to people you care about deeply?

3. What's the connection between loving someone and displaying love through actions?

4. You probably don't want to give flowers — or receive flowers — from everyone at church, so what are some real-life ways to show that you love and care about other Christians?

🗣 talk it over

When the real _____ meets real _____ for the right _____ in

the right _____, you have experienced _____ community.

Read Romans 12:9-13 as a group:

"Don't just pretend to love others. Really love them. Hate what is wrong. Hold tightly to what is good. Love each other with genuine affection, and take delight in honoring each other. Never be lazy, but work hard and serve the Lord enthusiastically. Rejoice in our confident hope. Be patient in trouble, and keep on praying. When God's people are in need, be ready to help them. Always be eager to practice hospitality."
Romans 12:9-13 (NLT)

This passage focuses on your relationship with other Christians

Why do many Christians pretend to love other Christians?

How do you know if you genuinely love another person? How easy or difficult is it for you to genuinely love other people?

Look at verse 11. Why does God care if we're lazy? How is it related to our spiritual maturity?

How easily do you practice patience during difficult times? How can prayer help you in those situations?

Think about the last time you served or helped a person in need. How did it feel? How would your life be different if you were constantly on the lookout for those opportunities?

What are some ways you can practice hospitality to other Christians? How can you become a more generous r12 Christian?

Does God care about our motives as long as our actions are good? Explain your answer.

"Playing church" isn't much fun. It's all about religious rules and regulations. It becomes mundane and boring. And ultimately, it will kill you spiritually.

Read Acts 5:1-11 as a group:

"But there was a certain man named Ananias who, with his wife, Sapphira, sold some property. He brought part of the money to the apostles, claiming it was the full amount. With his wife's consent, he kept the rest.
Then Peter said, ' Ananias, why have you let Satan fill your heart? You lied to the Holy Spirit, and you kept some of the money for yourself. The property was yours to sell or not sell, as you wished. And after selling it, the money was also yours to give away. How could you do a thing like this? You weren't lying to us but to God!'
As soon as Ananias heard these words, he fell to the floor and died. Everyone who heard about it was terrified. Then some young men got up, wrapped him in a sheet, and took him out and buried him.
About three hours later his wife came in, not knowing what had happened. Peter asked her, 'Was this the price you and your husband received for your land?'
'Yes,' she replied, 'that was the price.'
And Peter said, 'How could the two of you even think of conspiring to test the Spirit of the Lord like this? The young men who buried your husband are just outside the door, and they will carry you out, too.'
Instantly, she fell to the floor and died. When the young men came in and saw that she was dead, they carried her out and buried her beside her husband. Great fear gripped the entire church and everyone else who heard what had happened."
Acts 5:1-11 (NLT)

Why do you think God decided that the punishment for Ananias and Sapphira's lies would be death? What does that tell you about how much God values and rewards honesty?

Read John 13:34-35 as a group:

"So now I am giving you a new commandment: Love each other. Just as I have loved you, you should love each other. Your love for one another will prove to the world that you are my disciples."
John 13:34-35 (NLT)

Why is Christians' love for each other such a powerful witness and testimony to the world?

Pair up with another person in the group for this question:

Think about the Scripture passages we've discussed this week. What are some ways we can put these truths and instructions into practice in our youth group? How can you as teenagers lead the way in our church?

Come back together as a group to share answers to the previous question.

⊕ live it out

1. Read 1 Corinthians 13 every day.

2. Read days 26-30 of your daily devotional.

3. Look for a way this week to meet the needs of a friend or stranger. It can be a simple task, or it can be something you do every day for the next week. And if you want to take things to the next level, get together with some friends from your small group or youth ministry and volunteer in the community. Feed the homeless, clean up a community park, distribute coats and blankets to the needy, help at a nearby school — find some way to reach out and serve in love.

life isn't always fair

Today's Scripture

Bless those who persecute you. Don't curse them; pray that God will bless them. Be happy with those who are happy, and weep with those who weep. Live in harmony with each other. Don't be too proud to enjoy the company of ordinary people. And don't think you know it all!

Never pay back evil with more evil. Do things in such a way that everyone can see you are honorable. Do all that you can to live in peace with everyone.

Dear friends, never take revenge. Leave that to the righteous anger of God. For the Scriptures say, "I will take revenge; I will pay them back," says the Lord.

Instead, "If your enemies are hungry, feed them. If they are thirsty, give them something to drink. In doing this, you will heap burning coals of shame on their heads."

Don't let evil conquer you, but conquer evil by doing good.
Romans 12:14-21 (NLT)

Big Idea

With God's help, you can be prepared for rough, difficult, challenging moments in life.

Today's Thought

Maybe you've had a relatively "easy" life so far. Your parents are happily married, none of your close friends or relatives have died, you've experienced good health, and you've developed deep friendships with people you'll probably know for the rest of your life.

But maybe you've already gotten a firsthand lesson in how tough life can be. You've experienced times when circumstances went against you — and when people worked against you. You've been wronged and hurt and ignored and criticized. You've lost loved ones who helped shape your world. Your parents' marriage crumbled in front of your eyes.

Your friends may not even realize how painful and challenging your life has been — but God knows.

Bad things will happen to good people. How do you choose to **supernaturally** respond to the evil that is aimed at you?

In these verses from Romans 12, Paul is telling us to be ready for the "junk" in life. He encourages Christians to know how to respond in inevitable situations — times we want revenge against others, times we're persecuted for our faith, times we and our friends will weep and rejoice, times we will encounter evil.

This is really good news, in a way. It helps us avoid the temptation to run away from challenging situations or difficult people. We could read these verses and say, "OK, I'll just have two friends all of life, I'll move to a tiny town in the middle of nowhere, and I won't let the evil of this world get near me at all." Sorry. That strategy won't work.

That's why Paul's strategy — it's actually Jesus' strategy — is a better choice. Life isn't always fair. But as r12 Christians, our response to evil and difficulties and challenges can reveal God's work in our lives. And that's a pretty good path to travel.

Prayer
God, I'd like everything to work perfectly in my life, but I recognize this won't happen. Help me learn the spiritual lessons You want me to learn when I feel evil working against me. Give me Your strength to endure, and help me to become more like You through the whole process. Amen.

love your enemies

Today's Scripture

"You have heard the law that says, 'Love your neighbor' and hate your enemy. But I say, love your enemies! Pray for those who persecute you! In that way, you will be acting as true children of your Father in heaven. For he gives his sunlight to both the evil and the good, and he sends rain on the just and the unjust alike. If you love only those who love you, what reward is there for that? Even corrupt tax collectors do that much. If you are kind only to your friends, how are you different from anyone else? Even pagans do that.
Matthew 5:43-47 (NLT)

Big Idea

Do something revolutionary — love the people who hate you.

Today's Thought

OK, let's be honest — this commandment from Jesus in Matthew 5 has to be one of the hardest commandments in the Bible to obey! "God, you want me to love the people who hate me? Did you forget the fact that they HATE me?!"

Supernatural love is a difficult idea for us natural people to grasp, develop, and demonstrate. People who hurt us deserve punishment. People who betray us deserve retribution. That's just the way it should work, right?

But consider this: Why does God love us? Why *should* God love us? What can we possibly do to earn the affection of the Creator of the universe? (Try posting that one as your next status on Facebook and see what responses you get!) Yet somehow God loves you and me and every other person on the face of the earth. Incredible. That's what makes the song "Amazing Grace" so powerful to people of all ages — God's love for us is amazing and incomprehensible and illogical and powerful and immeasurable.

We as humans can never love as perfectly as God loves. But as r12 Christians, we are called to obey and love our enemies the way God loves them. It's a radical demonstration of what it means to follow Jesus. So how do we do it?

Start by forgiving the person who's hurt you. Make the *choice* to forgive. Keep making that choice as you move forward in the forgiveness process. And someday you may reach the place where you're happy when you hear that your enemy has succeeded and that God is blessing that person's life.

It won't happen overnight. But today you can begin the process of forgiveness and change and transformation — the process of loving your enemies.

Prayer

Dear God, I need Your help in following Jesus' command to love my enemies. You know that this is something I don't want to do, but I know it's a huge step in following You and becoming an r12 Christian. Give me Your strength today to forgive the people who've hurt me, and give me the strength to forgive them again tomorrow and the day after that and the day after that. Change my heart and my life. Amen.

Today's Scripture
Bless those who curse you. Pray for those who hurt you.
Luke 6:28

Big Idea
Do something else revolutionary — pray for the people who cause you pain.

Today's Thought
OK, if you thought yesterday's challenge was tough, today's isn't much easier! But it's really a "second step" in the process of desiring God's best for your enemies. Jesus told us to forgive the people who've hurt us — our enemies. But He also told us to pray for these same people. Why?

There's something powerful about prayer. It's good and healthy to see prayer as our ongoing conversation with God — but prayer also goes much deeper and holds such power to change our lives. And it's an essential practice in the process of loving our enemies.

Look at it this way: You've gone through a painful situation. A person you once called your friend has betrayed your trust, hurt your soul, and inflicted deep pain. Truly, this person has become your enemy. But then you read the words of Jesus: *Bless those who curse you. Pray for those who hurt you.* And your mind immediately thinks of this one person.

You make the decision to forgive. Each day, you wake up and ask for God's help in forgiving that person. But your feelings toward this enemy don't seem to change. You become angry and bitter every time you see or think about this person.

Prayer can help God's transforming work in your life. Pray for your enemy's salvation — or for God to help this person grow as a Christian. Pray for God's blessing in that person's life. Pray that this person would have the best year, best birthday, best class, best competition ever.

Maybe this sounds overly simple. But as you pray for God's best, your attitude will begin to change. Instead of being filled with anger or bitterness, you'll start experiencing compassion and concern. The change may not happen immediately, but your prayers will open the door to God's work in your life as an r12 Christian.

Jesus knew what He was talking about. He prayed for the people who persecuted, rejected, and crucified Him. Let prayer for your enemies be the spark of change and transformation in your life.

Prayer

God, I don't really know how to pray for the best in my enemies' lives, but Jesus did it for His enemies, and I want to become more like Jesus. Give me inspiration and ideas on what to pray for, and help my heart to change as I seek Your best for my enemies' lives. Amen.

Today's Scripture
Don't say, "I will get even for this wrong." Wait for the Lord to handle the matter.
Proverbs 20:22

Big Idea
Let God decide if people deserve revenge — it's His job, not yours.

Today's Thought
Your brothers betrayed you and sold you into a life of slavery. People you met along the way failed to deliver on their promises. You were accused of wrongdoing — even though you were innocent.

If this were you, you'd have a lot of reasons to be bitter and angry. You'd want revenge, retaliation, and payback. Most people would say you were justified.

Not God.

In the Old Testament, a guy named Joseph went through those very experiences, yet when he had the opportunity to get revenge, he said "no thanks" and chose to let God take care of things. Check out Genesis 42 through 45 for the full story of how Joseph handled himself when his brothers — unaware of his true identity — ask for food in the middle of a famine. Joseph easily could have retaliated by letting his brothers and their families starve. But he didn't.

Joseph isn't the only biblical character who accurately understood God's perspective on revenge. King Saul persecuted and pursued David, but when David had the chance to kill Saul, he didn't do it (1 Samuel 24 and 26). When early church leader Stephen was being stoned to death (Acts 7), he prayed that God would forgive his accusers.

And the greatest example was Jesus on the cross — he prayed for forgiveness instead of asking God for revenge against the people responsible for His crucifixion (Luke 23:34).

God doesn't want us to take revenge because it's not our job — it's His job to judge. And besides, revenge rarely solves problems. It almost always escalates the situation!

You're never more like God than when you as an r12 Christian reject revenge and choose to supernaturally conquer evil by doing good.

Prayer
God, there are so many times I want to retaliate against the people who have hurt me. You see inside my mind and heart, and You know how I'm still struggling to forgive them for what they've done. Help me to follow Your path. Help me to trust You because I know You want the best for my life and You've got my back. Amen.

Today's Scripture

We think you ought to know, dear brothers and sisters, about the trouble we went through in the province of Asia. We were crushed and overwhelmed beyond our ability to endure, and we thought we would never live through it. In fact, we expected to die. But as a result, we stopped relying on ourselves and learned to rely only on God, who raises the dead. And he did rescue us from mortal danger, and he will rescue us again. We have placed our confidence in him, and he will continue to rescue us.
2 Corinthians 1:8-10 (NLT)

Big Idea

Relying on yourself is a recipe for spiritual death, but relying on God brings spiritual life.

Today's Thought

Ever heard the story of *The Little Engine That Could*? It's a classic tale for kids about a little engine that climbed a high mountain because it had a positive attitude and kept repeating the phrase "I think I can, I think I can." It's a great story to teach young children about the importance of hard work and dedication. But is it a good strategy for spiritual growth?

Look at 2 Corinthians 1:9. Paul makes a fascinating statement: "We stopped relying on ourselves and learned to rely only on God." Wow! Paul didn't think he could — in fact, he *knew* he couldn't without God's help.

You will become a radical example of a changed life as you stop relying on yourself and learn to rely only on God. When we rely on ourselves, we become tired and frustrated because of our human limitations. When we rely on God, we have the opportunity to tap into a limitless source of strength and creativity and inspiration and encouragement and transformation.

That's what it means to be an r12 Christian. Relying on God means being **surrendered** to God, **separate** from the world and its values, **sober** in self-assessment, **serving** in love, and **supernaturally** responsive to evil with good.

Perhaps we can take The Little Engine's idea and adapt it: I think I can — rely more and more on God! I think I can — become an r12 Christian as you work in my life! I think I can — become a radical example of a changed life!

Prayer

God, You're so much more powerful than I am, and nothing is impossible for You. Help me learn how to rely on you every day for answers and protection and transformation. I want to become a radical example of a changed life, but I know that only happens as I become more like You. Make me into a growing, healthy, authentic r12 Christian who is rooted in a deep relationship with You. Amen.

students

Overcoming the Evil Aimed at You

Supernaturally responding to evil with good (Romans 12:14-21)

think about it

Enemies don't deserve forgiveness or mercy or love. Enemies deserve revenge and payback and retribution. That's the way it works in our world. If you've been hurt, find the person who did it and strike back.

But as r12 Christians, we're called to make different choices. Of course, "different" doesn't always mean "easy." It's tough to forgive the people who've hurt, abandoned, betrayed, and gossiped about us. Yet God calls us to take that huge step and forgive. It's part of His call to supernaturally overcome evil with good.

REVIEW

1. Last week's small group lesson focused on *serving* others in love as r12 Christians. We talked about the importance of having a genuine, authentic love for other Christians and the impact this love can have on the world around us. Your challenges at the end of the lesson included reading 1 Corinthians 13 every day and meeting the needs of a stranger or friend — or working together with friends to meet a need in the community.

2. Your devotional readings this week focused on *supernaturally* responding to evil with good. You read about preparing for tough times in life, loving the people who hate you, praying for the people who've caused you pain, rejecting revenge and retaliation, and becoming a radical example of a changed life.

get it started

Opening Question
How many hours or minutes have you gone without sinning in your life? How often do you need to experience forgiveness?

Interactive Opening
1. Are these some crimes or events that are beyond forgiveness? Is it possible some people have done something so bad that they don't deserve forgiveness? Explain your answer.

2. How do you typically respond when someone does something that hurts you? Do you immediately look for a way to retaliate, or do you withdraw? Why?

3. What do you think Jesus would say to the person we read about in this news event? How would He approach the situation?

🗣 talk it over

Read Romans 12:14-21 as a group:

"Bless those who persecute you. Don't curse them; pray that God will bless them. Be happy with those who are happy, and weep with those who weep. Live in harmony with each other. Don't be too proud to enjoy the company of ordinary people. And don't think you know it all!
Never pay back evil with more evil. Do things in such a way that everyone can see you are honorable. Do all that you can to live in peace with everyone.
Dear friends, never take revenge. Leave that to the righteous anger of God. For the Scriptures say, 'I will take revenge; I will pay them back,' says the Lord.
Instead, 'If your enemies are hungry, feed them. If they are thirsty, give them something to drink. In doing this, you will heap burning coals of shame on their heads.'
Don't let evil conquer you, but conquer evil by doing good."
Romans 12:14-21 (NLT)

This passage focuses on your relationship to non-believers

These are some pretty powerful verses — and may feel overwhelming to actually live out! What's your initial response to reading and hearing these words from the Apostle Paul?

Think of a recent time when you've forgiven another person — or when someone has forgiven you. What impact did this experience have on you?

What if you're dealing with a situation where YOU have caused an issue, even though you see the other person as an enemy? How should you handle this situation?

When do you find it easy to forgive? When do you find it difficult? What's the difference?

What would our world look like if everyone always took revenge on the people who caused hurt and pain? What do you think it would be like to live in a world where everyone acted that way?

In Romans 12, Paul offers three steps we as r12 Christians can walk through as we supernaturally respond to the people who have hurt us:

1. Choose to _____ them

Release your desire for payback and vengeance. Ask God for help as you take this step. You won't feel like forgiving the person; it's a decision you make. And as we talked about in this past week's devotional readings, it may take a long time to reach the second and third steps in this process.

2. Choose to _____ with them

It's easy to weep, rejoice, mourn, and celebrate with our friends. But with our enemies? That's tough! But as you work through the process of forgiveness, you will find times when you realize your attitudes and emotions have changed. You no longer want revenge against this person; you want God to bless and save and redeem this person.

3. Consider opportunities to _____ with them

Depending on the situation, this may or may not be possible. Sometimes we simply need to forgive and move forward with life. But other times, we have opportunities to live at peace with our former enemies because we've turned the situation over to God. We've decided to let Him handle whatever consequences are necessary.

It's important to remember that Paul's words in this passage echo the same ideas Jesus taught people.

Read Matthew 5:43-48 as a group:

"You have heard the law that says, 'Love your neighbor' and hate your enemy. But I say, love your enemies! Pray for those who persecute you! In that way, you will be acting as true children of your Father in heaven. For he gives his sunlight to both the evil and the good, and he sends rain on the just and the unjust alike. If you love only those who love you, what reward is there for that? Even corrupt tax collectors do that much. If you are kind only to your friends, how are you different from anyone else? Even pagans do that. But you are to be perfect, even as your Father in heaven is perfect."
Matthew 5:43-48 (NLT)

Look at verse 44. What kinds of prayers might you pray for people who persecute you? How would those prayers be different from the way you pray for your closest friends?

Verse 47 says Christians who are only kind to their friends really aren't different from people who don't claim to follow Christ. How does it make you feel to hear and read those words from Jesus?

If we try to do all of these things in our own energy — without seeking and

relying on God's strength — what are some of the likely results, and why?

Jesus' instruction to love and pray for your enemies is one of the greatest statements He made — and He backed it up with action, asking God to forgive His enemies while He was hanging on the Cross.

Closing Activity
Think about someone who has caused you pain because of hurt, rejection, gossip, or some other unfair action. This person doesn't deserve forgiveness, but you believe God wants you to forgive this person as a decision that can help you grow spiritually and become an even more mature r12 Christian.

live it out

1. Re-read Romans 12 and highlight or circle the words and phrases that have had the greatest impact on you during this small group series.

2. Look back at the prayer journal you started keeping in the first week of this small group series. What prayers has God answered? What are you continuing to pray about each day? Give God thanks for the answers that have arrived — and the answers He will provide in the days and weeks ahead.

3. Journal about what it means to live a life that is totally surrendered to God. How will you continue to grow in this area, now that your small group has finished this series?

How do you become a Christian?

The most incredible decision you can ever make in your life is the decision to follow Jesus. If you've haven't already made that choice, this is your chance to begin the journey and make the first step of "surrender" in your life. It means surrendering your past mistakes — what the Bible calls sin — to Jesus as your Savior, and it means surrendering today and the future to Jesus as your Lord.

So, what does it mean when people talk about "receiving salvation" through Jesus?

Back at the beginning of the Bible, we learn that God created humanity in His image (*Genesis 1:27*). The first man and woman were created as perfect beings, but they made the decision to disobey God and sin (*Genesis 3*). This ruptured the divine, perfect relationship God wanted to experience with humanity.

Throughout the Old Testament — the first part of the Bible — men and women could only pay for their sins through sacrifices of animals. The blood of these animals would cover the people's sins, but it was a temporary solution. One sacrifice would not cover the sins of a person or nation for eternity.

You and I continue to sin (*Romans 3:23*). It's part of our human, fallen nature. No one can live a life that is good enough or perfect enough to earn entry into heaven and eternity in God's presence.

But instead of asking us to sacrifice animals to pay for our sins, God provided a permanent solution through Jesus Christ. Jesus was both fully God and fully human; He lived a perfect, sinless life (*1 Peter 2:22*). He then became the ideal sacrifice for us when He died on the cross — and on the third day He came back to life.

On our own, we will continue to experience separation from God, but we have the opportunity to receive the gift of salvation that Jesus provided through His sacrifice on the cross. *"For the wages of sin is death, but the free gift of God is eternal life through Christ Jesus our Lord"* (*Romans 6:23*).

God has an incredible dream for your life, and the amazing journey begins with salvation! If you want to make the decision to follow Jesus, we'd encourage you to pray this simple prayer:

Jesus, I thank you for the gift of salvation you've made available to me. I've messed up so many times on my own. I need your help in my life. Please forgive me of my sins. I receive your gift of forgiveness and eternal life. I want you to be my Savior and my Lord. I want to follow you for the rest of my life. And I ask this in your name, amen.

Sweet! Make sure you tell someone about the decision you've made to become a Christian. You can tell your small group leader, your parents, your youth pastor, your best friends, your friends at school — or all of those people! Stay connected with your church's youth ministry and a small group, and spend time exploring the Bible. We recommend that you find a translation of the Bible that's easy to understand, such as the New Living Translation or the New International Version. We're praying for God's best in your life, and we know you'll experience an incredible journey as you become an authentic, mature r12 Christian!

If you have more questions about starting a relationship with God, you can explore those answers online at *LivingontheEdge.org/newstart*.

LEADER'S GUIDE

o12
students
small group
study guide

LEADER'S GUIDE

Thanks! We're excited about your willingness to lead a small group through this exploration of what it means to be an r12 Christian. Please know that our team is praying for your personal growth and success — and for a successful time with your students!

This guide is designed to help you, the leader, effectively walk through these six lessons with your students. Please take time to review each lesson before meeting with your students. You may think of personal illustrations or examples that will enhance the conversation. You also may generate some solid follow-up questions that you can have prepared before your group meets. You may need to revise or edit questions, based on the age and background of your students. Do whatever it takes to make this resource helpful for your teens!

You'll discover that we've written out various passages of Scripture in each lesson. We want students to bring their own Bibles, but we know that not all will for every lesson. Encourage your students to still bring their Bibles each week, and if they have a variety of translations, invite them to read how their Bibles interpret the same passage.

Here is a brief explanation of each section in the lessons:

GET IT STARTED

This section includes an Opening Question and an Interactive Opening (with the exception of Week 1). The Opening Question is a short, simple icebreaker to get your students talking and interacting. The Interactive Opening requires a little work on your part to gather or assemble items to help your students learn visually. Use one or both — or adapt them to fit the needs of your small group.

REVIEW

This section offers a brief recap of the previous week's small group lesson and readings from the devotional guide.

TALK IT OUT

This section includes a series of questions designed to stimulate conversation among your students. It also features at least one Scripture passage — usually multiple passages — for discussion and examination. You'll see that many of our questions are open-ended — in other words, your teenagers will be asked to think about their answers instead of simply replying "yes" or "no." We believe this can encourage spiritual growth because it requires young people to think through what it means to follow Jesus, instead of offering canned or predictable answers. The Leaders Guide includes ALL of the questions and SOME suggested answers. Many of the questions don't require explanations or suggestions, but in some cases we've provided some possible answers or direction for the conversation.

LIVE IT OUT

This section offers some take-away challenges for your students. Most weeks, the list will include Scripture readings for the upcoming week, along with opportunities for your teenagers to apply what you've discussed.

What is True Spirituality?

think about it

You're a teenager, which means you like to dream. You dream about the future. You dream about life's opportunities. You dream about places you'll visit and people you'll meet. You dream about your first job and first car and meeting the perfect spouse and buying a house and starting a family — it's an endless list for most teenagers.

God has dreams and desires for your life, too. Maybe you'd never thought of it before, but it's true. God wants you to love Him, to spend time with Him, to reflect His characteristics, to care for others, to become more like Jesus, and to authentically display your faith. That's God's dream — that you and I would live like r12 Christians.

get it started

[NOTE: We do not have a specific opening activity suggested for this lesson. We encourage you to begin your time together by asking students to reveal their quirkiest personality trait or favorite pizza toppings or least favorite sport to watch on TV or most frustrating store at the mall — anything to get the teenagers comfortable. If you're working with a group of students who've already been together as a small group, talk about how their lives have been going since you last met.]

The New Testament — especially the Gospels of Matthew, Mark, Luke, and John — talk a lot about Jesus and His disciples. What does the word "disciple" mean to you?

If you hear someone talking about "spiritual maturity," what does that phrase mean to you?

Pair up with another person in the group and take a couple of minutes to answer this question:
What are some signs or pieces of evidence you would see in the life of someone who is a spiritually mature follower of Jesus?

[NOTE: Your students may go toward the "easy" answers of "attending church" or "reading the Bible," but encourage them to think deeper about how

Come back together as a group to discuss your answers to the previous question.

For the next few weeks, our small group is embarking on an adventure to discover what it means to be r12 Christians. Think of it as a voyage into new terrain, an expedition on a spiritual journey God has planned for you. Romans 12 will be your guidebook — or roadmap, if you like that image.

Read Romans 12 as a group:

"And so, dear brothers and sisters, I plead with you to give your bodies to God because of all he has done for you. Let them be a living and holy sacrifice—the kind he will find acceptable. This is truly the way to worship him.
Don't copy the behavior and customs of this world, but let God transform you into a new person by changing the way you think. Then you will learn to know God's will for you, which is good and pleasing and perfect.
Because of the privilege and authority God has given me, I give each of you this warning: Don't think you are better than you really are. Be honest in your evaluation of yourselves, measuring yourselves by the faith God has given us. ⁴Just as our bodies have many parts and each part has a special function, ⁵so it is with Christ's body. We are many parts of one body, and we all belong to each other.
In his grace, God has given us different gifts for doing certain things well. So if God has given you the ability to prophesy, speak out with as much faith as God has given you. If your gift is serving others, serve them well. If you are a teacher, teach well. If your gift is to encourage others, be encouraging. If it is giving, give generously. If God has given you leadership ability, take the responsibility seriously. And if you have a gift for showing kindness to others, do it gladly.
Don't just pretend to love others. Really love them. Hate what is wrong. Hold tightly to what is good. Love each other with genuine affection, and take delight in honoring each other. Never be lazy, but work hard and serve the Lord enthusiastically. Rejoice in our confident hope. Be patient in trouble, and keep on praying. When God's people are in need, be ready to help them. Always be eager to practice hospitality.
Bless those who persecute you. Don't curse them; pray that God will bless them. Be happy with those who are happy, and weep with those who weep. Live in harmony with each other. Don't be too proud to enjoy the company of ordinary people. And don't think you know it all!
Never pay back evil with more evil. Do things in such a way that everyone can see you are honorable. Do all that you can to live in peace with everyone.
Dear friends, never take revenge. Leave that to the righteous anger of God. For the Scriptures say, "I will take revenge; I will pay them back," says the Lord.
Instead, "If your enemies are hungry, feed them. If they are thirsty, give them something to drink. In doing this, you will heap burning coals of shame on their

heads."
Don't let evil conquer you, but conquer evil by doing good."
Romans 12:1-21 (NLT)

This passage of Scripture provides an incredible summary of what it means to be an r12 Christian. And these verses help us understand five kinds of relationships we have in our lives. An r12 Christian is growing in all of these areas:

Your relationship with <u>God</u>
> This grows when you are *Surrendered to God* (v. 1)

Your relationship with the <u>world</u>
> This grows when you are *Separate from the world* (v. 2)

Your relationship with <u>yourself</u>
> This grows when you are *Sober in self-assessment* (v. 3-8)

Your relationship with <u>other Christians</u>
> This grows when you are *Serving in love* (v. 9-13)

Your relationship to <u>non-believers</u>
> This grows when you are *Supernaturally responding to evil with good* (v. 14-21)

[NOTE: The underlined words represent fill-ins from the student version.]

This kind of mature Christianity is relational. It's not performance driven, and it's not about religious rules and regulations.

Unfortunately, a lot of Christians seem to be heading in a different direction. We talk a good game, but aren't fulfilling God's dream for us. Some people call it "Consumer Christianity" or "Cultural Christianity" — in other words, what's in it for me? This breaks God's heart.

talk it over

How have your dreams about the future changed since you were a kid?
[NOTE: Consider talking about the dreams YOU had as an elementary-age kid and how those changed with time — or how they stayed the same!]

Do you spend more time thinking about WHAT you will do when you grow up or WHO you will become when you grow up? What's the difference between those two questions, and which do you think God wants you to do more?

[NOTE: The goal with this question is to emphasize that God cares more about who we are than what we do. Our culture places a lot of emphasis on the WHAT and not enough on the WHO of becoming a mature adult.]

What's the significance of being the KIND of person God desires?
[NOTE: You might want to reference 1 Samuel 16:7, when God tells the prophet Samuel that He cares more about a person's heart than appearance.]

What are some specific dreams you believe God has for your life?

Can you be a Christian without being an authentic follower of Jesus? Explain your answer.
[NOTE: This question could spur some debate and conversation. Be careful that it doesn't turn in the direction of being judgmental toward others. But the key idea is that some people may claim to be a Christian without living a fully surrendered life to God — or seeking ways to become more like Jesus. That doesn't mean this person won't go to Heaven — only God knows for sure — but this person's life on earth may have less fulfillment and impact than what God desires.]

Pair up with another person in the group for the next couple of questions:
What words would you use to describe your relationship with God right now?
[NOTE: You're looking for adjectives — descriptive words. If the group is small enough or you feel comfortable enough as a leader, consider follow-up questions about WHY a student is feeling a certain way in their relationship with God.]

How have you grown spiritually in the last few weeks?
> **How about in the last six months?**
> **How about in the last year?**

Come back together as a group for this final question:
What people have had the biggest impact on your spiritual life, and how did they play that role?

live it out

[NOTE: Challenge your students to follow these application steps in the next week.]

1. Read Romans 12 every day.

2. Read days 6-10 of your daily devotional.

3. Keep a prayer journal and write down your prayers, if you don't already do this; you'll be able to see how God is working in your life.

[NOTE: Consider ending your small group with a time of prayer for each other, or you as the leader may choose to be the only person praying aloud. Nudge your students out of their comfort zones when it comes to prayer — but don't push them off the deep end.]

Giving God What He Wants the Most

Surrender to God (Romans 12:1)

think about it

Want to stir things up and create a buzz among your friends? Change your relationship status on Facebook or MySpace. You'll get inundated with comments and text messages asking for all the details.

Beginning a friendship with God can create a buzz, too — but God wants to be more than just your friend. In fact, God's ideal "status relationship" with you would be summed up in this word: surrendered. It's one word that describes the kind of relationship God wants with each of us — our relationship with Him as r12 Christians. He's already sent you a request to change your status — are you willing to respond?

REVIEW

1. Last week's small group lesson focused on the "big picture" of being an r12 Christian. We saw how this one passage of Scripture examines our relationships with God, the world, ourselves, other Christians, and non-believers. Your challenges at the end of the lesson included reading Romans 12 every day this week and starting a prayer journal.

2. Your devotional readings this week focused on *surrendering* everything to God. You read about becoming a living sacrifice, having the right attitude toward surrender, leaving behind your selfish ways, recognizing the rewards of surrender, and preparing for a life that will never be the same.

get it started

Opening Question

Imagine being Facebook friends with God. What word would you choose to define your current relationship status with God? Why that word?
[NOTE: Possible answers could include "Struggling," "Surrendered," "Unsure," "It's Complicated," and so on.]

Interactive Opening

[NOTE: Before your small group meets, grab some newspapers or magazines from home. Ask your students to look through the articles and try to find people who are examples of our culture's standards of "success." Then ask some or all of the five questions we've included in the student version of this lesson.]

1. Why are the people in these newspaper and magazine articles considered successful?

2. Is their success lasting, or will it quickly fade away? Explain your opinion.

3. What are some of the ways our culture defines success — including success for teenagers? How much does the idea of *surrendering* fit into the cultural view of success?

4. How do you think these examples of success line up with God's perspective on success? Is this what God wants from your life?

5. How might God explain His definition of success? What role do you think surrendering plays in his definition?

talk it over

Read Romans 12:1 as a group:

"And so, dear brothers and sisters, I plead with you to give your bodies to God because of all he has done for you. Let them be a living and holy sacrifice—the kind he will find acceptable. This is truly the way to worship him."
Romans 12:1 (NLT)

This verse focuses on your relationship with God.

What do you think it means to be a "living and holy sacrifice"?

How can a surrendered life be a way to worship God?
[NOTE: By giving everything to God, it's a display of our trust and faith in God — we honor God by focusing everything on Him. That's worship.]

Why does God want us to offer our lives as sacrifices? Why doesn't He simply force us to follow and obey Him?

What does it look like, specifically, to be surrendered to God?
[NOTE: A surrendered life is built around honoring God and placing God as the highest priority above everyone and everything else.]

What kinds of religious games do Christians sometimes play with their faith, with God, and with other Christians?

What's the difference between saying you're a Christian and living like one?

Read Matthew 13:44-46 as a group:

The Kingdom of Heaven is like a treasure that a man discovered hidden in a field. In his excitement, he hid it again and sold everything he owned to get enough money to buy the field.
Again, the Kingdom of Heaven is like a merchant on the lookout for choice pearls. When he discovered a pearl of great value, he sold everything he owned and bought it!"
Matthew 13:44-46 (NLT)

Romans 12:1 describes surrendering as a reasonable sacrifice to God. In these parables, we read about two people who gave up everything so they could acquire something of greater value. Their friends might have thought they were foolish, but they were actually wise: They surrendered "second best" and received the "best of all."

Jesus used these two brief parables to teach a crowd of people about the importance of placing God's priorities first in our lives. God wants us to seek Him and His kingdom as the most valuable treasure we could pursue. What are some modern examples that would illustrate the same idea Jesus communicated?

Do you tend to think of "surrender" as being something negative or something positive? Why?
[NOTE: Ask students to refer to their reading from Day 4 if they don't have any answers to this question. It talks about how surrender is worth the cost we pay.]

Read Psalm 84:11 as a group:

"For the Lord God is our sun and our shield. He gives us grace and glory. The Lord will withhold no good thing from those who do what is right."
Psalm 84:11 (NLT)

What does Psalm 84:11 tell you about God's character?

Pair up with another person in the group for these questions:
What areas of your life have you surrendered to God? How did you reach the place where you could make that decision?

What are some of the challenges you face in fully surrendering your life to God? How can we work together and hold each other accountable to grow in this area?

Surrender is the channel through which God's best and biggest blessings flow. God is waiting for us to go "all in" with our lives — total surrender to Him.

That's the first step to experiencing God's greatness in your life. Are you all in? The answer is either yes or no.

live it out

[NOTE: Challenge your students to follow these application steps in the next week.]

1. Read Genesis 12, which was mentioned in Day 5 of your Student Devotional Guide. It's the story of how God called Abraham to make an incredible sacrifice in his life.

2. Read days 11-15 of your daily devotional.

3. Journal about the idea of going "all in" with your life. What does this mean to you as an r12 Christian? How can you do it? How can other people help you in this process?

[NOTE: Consider ending your small group with a time of prayer for each other, or you as the leader, may choose to be the only person praying aloud. Nudge your students out of their comfort zones when it comes to prayer — but don't push them off the deep end.]

Getting God's Very Best

Separate from the world's values (Romans 12:2)

think about it

It can be tough to live a healthy lifestyle in this country. We're busy, we have numerous responsibilities, and sometimes it's just so tough to say "no" to that super large soda, that extra-rich dessert, or that deep-dish pizza. But to remain healthy physically, we need to be aware of the consequences our nutritional habits have on our bodies.

If we aren't doing so well with our physical nutrition, it's likely we'll hear about it on our next visit to the doctor! But what about our "spiritual" diets? What does it mean to pursue spiritual health as an r12 Christian? And is it even possible living in this culture?

REVIEW

1. Last week's small group lesson focused on *surrendering* everything to God as r12 Christians. We talked about what it means to be a living sacrifice for God and how surrender is the channel through which God's best and biggest blessings flow. Your challenges at the end of the lesson included reading Genesis 12 and journaling about what it means to go "all in" as an r12 Christian.

2. Your devotional readings this week focused on being separate from the world's values. You read about choosing to love God instead of the world's ways, eating a "spiritually nutritious" diet, preparing for the battle in your mind, knowing your areas of weakness, and following five tips for renewing your mind.

get it started

Opening Question
Several verses in the Bible talk about "eating" God's truth or seeing God's Word as something we can consume (including Jeremiah 15:16, Ezekiel 3:1-3, and Revelation 10:9-10.) What do you think this idea means? How is it relevant to you today?

[NOTE: Obviously, God doesn't want us to physically consume pieces of the Bible — but we can "digest" and "absorb" the spiritually rich nutrients of Scripture.]

[NOTE: Before your small group meets, gather some to-go menus from restaurants in your area. Try to get a mix of menus, if possible — fast food joints, chain restaurants, hole-in-the-wall restaurants, sandwich shops, and hometown delis. Ask your students to review the food options on the menus before asking them the four questions we've included in the student version of this lesson.]

1. Where might you go if you wanted the tastiest meals, and why? What if you wanted the *healthiest* meals, and why?

2. At your age, you might not think much about the nutritional value of the food you eat. Why will this matter more as you get older?

3. What might be some similarities and parallels between physical food and spiritual food?

4. How spiritually healthy are you right now? If you don't know, how might you figure out an answer to that question?

talk it over

What do you think is the difference between making a decision to follow Jesus and then becoming a disciple of Jesus?
[NOTE: Making the decision is a first step that provides salvation, but becoming a disciple — an r12 Christian — is a process of growth, change, and commitment.]

Read Romans 12:2 as a group:

"Don't copy the behavior and customs of this world, but let God transform you into a new person by changing the way you think. Then you will learn to know God's will for you, which is good and pleasing and perfect."
Romans 12:2 (NLT)

This verse focuses on your relationship with the world.

Why do many Christians copy or imitate the behavior and patterns and choices of our world and culture? What are some consequences if we do this?

Why and how does changing the way you think contribute to God's work of transformation in your life?
[NOTE: So much of our behavior is rooted in how we think of ourselves and the world around us. The more we can think about things the way God does,

the more our lives will reflect His goals and values.]

Paul wrote that God's will for you is good and pleasing and perfect. What does each of those three words mean to you, and what emotions do they evoke?

What words would you use to describe the experience of choosing to go your own direction and ignoring God's will?
[NOTE: Most students will offer brief answers, and that's OK on this question.]

What does Romans 12:2 tell you about the process of change and spiritual growth? How much responsibility falls on God's shoulders and how much falls on your shoulders as an r12 Christian?
[NOTE: This is a fascinating topic that you might want to explore deeper if you have an older, more mature group. We know that God is the only one who can change and transform us — yet the Bible makes it clear that we do our part, too. It's similar to the idea of us preparing the ground and God causing growth to occur. Both parts are necessary — but again, we don't create spiritual growth - that's God's job.]

Last week, we talked about the importance of surrendering everything to God. How does this fit into the ideas of being separate from the world and renewing our minds?
[NOTE: Surrendering everything includes surrendering the things we think and the way we think.]

If you've read the devotional guide this past week, you're already familiar with these five tips for renewing your mind as an r12 Christian:

Read God's Word
"God blesses the one who reads the words of this prophecy to the church, and he blesses all who listen to its message and obey what it says, for the time is near."
Revelation 1:3 (NLT)

Hear God's Word
"Consequently, faith comes from hearing the message, and the message is heard through the word about Christ."
Romans 10:17 (TNIV)

Study God's Word
"Work hard so you can present yourself to God and receive his approval. Be a good worker, one who does not need to be ashamed and who correctly explains the word of truth."
2 Timothy 2:15 (NLT)

Memorize God's Word
"I have hidden your word in my heart, that I might not sin against you."
Psalm 119:11 (NLT)

Meditate on God's Word
"Study this Book of Instruction continually. Meditate on it day and night so you will be sure to obey everything written in it. Only then will you prosper and succeed in all you do."
Joshua 1:8 (NLT)

[NOTE: The underlined words represent fill-ins from the student version.]

Read 1 John 2:15-17 as a group:

"Do not love this world nor the things it offers you, for when you love the world, you do not have the love of the Father in you. For the world offers only a craving for physical pleasure, a craving for everything we see, and pride in our achievements and possessions. These are not from the Father, but are from this world. And this world is fading away, along with everything that people crave. But anyone who does what pleases God will live forever."
1 John 2:15-17 (NLT)

Verse 16 tells us about three passions Satan uses against us. They're actually God-given desires, but Satan's goal is to twist and distort them into passions that we pursue in the wrong way and with the wrong motives — and that displeases God:

Passion to <u>feel</u> — lust of flesh

Passion to <u>have</u> — lust of eyes

Passion to <u>be</u> — pride of life

[NOTE: The underlined words represent fill-ins from the student version.]

What are some specific ways Satan might go after teenagers with these three areas of temptation?

Pair up with another person in the group for this question:
You probably spend a lot of time thinking about the food you enjoy eating. How about spiritual food? What kinds of "food" would help you grow as an r12 Christian? How are you doing with your "spiritual nutritional habits" right now, and what are some specific steps you can take to grow in this area?

Come back together as a group to share some of your answers to the previous question.

live it out

[NOTE: Challenge your students to follow these application steps in the next week.]

1. Choose one of the five tips for renewing your mind we discussed in this lesson, and practice one of them every day this week. Journal about this experience, and see what God reveals to you and how He challenges you through this practice.

2. Read days 16-20 of your daily devotional.

3. Take a NO/YES challenge. Say "no" to something in your life — maybe take a media fast this week from Facebook or video games or your favorite TV shows. Say "yes" to using that time each day to read your Bible, pray, journal, listen to worship music, or reflect on God.

[NOTE: Consider ending your small group with a time of prayer for each other, or you as the leader, may choose to be the only person praying aloud. Nudge your students out of their comfort zones when it comes to prayer — but don't push them off the deep end.]

Coming to Grips with the Real You

Sober in self-assessment (Romans 12:3-8)

think about it

OK, let's be honest: If you spend all day walking around and talking to yourself out loud, you will get some odd stares from people. It just isn't considered right. But every day, you have conversations in your head — self-talk about how you see yourself, how others might be seeing you at that moment, if your breath smells OK, if you're going to see that person you have the biggest crush on, and if your hair looks just right.

Sometimes we're too critical about ourselves. And sometimes we think too highly about who we really are. God says we need to walk the middle road: Recognize and appreciate strengths and weaknesses, and pursue a path that honors the unique way God has created each of us. God wants us to think humbly about ourselves. In other words, as an r12 Christian, you're called to not think too highly or too lowly of yourself — to simply not focus on yourself but to think of God and others.

REVIEW

1. Last week's small group lesson focused on being *separate* from the world's values as r12 Christians. We talked about ways Satan will attack our thoughts, and we discussed five strategies for renewing the mind: reading, hearing, studying, memorizing, and meditating on God's Word. Your challenges at the end of the lesson included practicing one of those five strategies during the week and taking a NO/YES challenge — fasting from an activity to spend more time with God.

2. Your devotional readings this week focused on having a *sober* and honest evaluation of yourself. You read about recognizing that God gave you strengths and weaknesses, finding your true identity, experiencing true security, discovering true significance, and becoming a world-class you.

get it started

Opening Question

What is a career or achievement or award that you'd like to accomplish or reach, but you know it probably won't happen because you simply aren't created or wired in the right way?

[NOTE: Examples would including "I want to win American Idol, but I really can't sing well at all" or "I'd like to be an NBA star, but both of my parents are just 5'4" tall" or "I want to display my art at the world's greatest museums, but my stick figure drawings don't even look like stick figures."]

Interactive Opening
[NOTE: Bring some fake money with you to this week's small group. It could be some cash from your Monopoly game or some cheesy cash you buy in the toy aisle at your local Wal-Mart. Also bring along some real cash — maybe even a bunch of fresh $1 bills from your bank. Give your students a chance to look at the fake and the real money, and then ask them the four questions we've included in the student version of this lesson.]

1. Why do some people fall victim to counterfeit money?

2. How can you know the difference between real money and counterfeit money?

3. What are some genuine things that the devil tries to counterfeit? Why does he choose those things?

4. How can you protect yourself from spiritually counterfeit things?

[NOTE: Remind your students that Satan has a system set up that provides counterfeit ways for finding significance, security, happiness and fulfillment. These are things God placed in our hearts, but the devil offers lies about how to find these things. It's shiny and attractive and it tastes good for a while — but then it becomes sour.]

talk it over

What kind of "self talk" do you have most days? What are some ways your "self talk" guide your choices, actions, and attitudes throughout the day?

Read Romans 12:3-8 as a group:

"Because of the privilege and authority God has given me, I give each of you this warning: Don't think you are better than you really are. Be honest in your evaluation of yourselves, measuring yourselves by the faith God has given us. Just as our bodies have many parts and each part has a special function, so it is with Christ's body. We are many parts of one body, and we all belong to each other. In his grace, God has given us different gifts for doing certain things well. So if God has given you the ability to prophesy, speak out with as much faith as God has given you. If your gift is serving others, serve them well. If you are a teacher, teach well. If your gift is to encourage others, be encouraging. If it is giving,

give generously. If God has given you leadership ability, take the responsibility seriously. And if you have a gift for showing kindness to others, do it gladly." Romans 12:3-8 (NLT)

This passage focuses on your relationship with yourself.

Verse 3 says that as r12 Christians, we need to have an "honest" evaluation of ourselves; other translations of the Bible use the word "sober." What's one area of your life where you've thought you were better than you really were? And what's an area where you didn't think of yourself as being as talented as you really were?

How do you handle this balancing act — recognizing your weaknesses and your strengths without becoming negative OR filled with pride?

What does it mean that all Christians "belong to each other," as Paul says in verse 5?

How would you summarize Paul's main point in verses 6 through 8?

Why do you think Paul decided to highlight these specific spiritual gifts?

Why are we happier talking to other people about our strengths but not our weaknesses — yet when we're alone, we sometimes become obsessed with those weaknesses?

What's so difficult about letting down our guard and revealing the real person inside? What are the risks, and what are the possible rewards? Let's talk about this for a few minutes.
[NOTE: Depending on your group, this could be a good question for some deep, challenging, revealing conversation. Some students may choose to talk in generalities, while others may decide to let down their guard and reveal their true selves. If students share deep personal information, remind everyone else of the value of confidentiality and maintaining each others' confidence in a small group.]

We sometimes compensate for areas where we feel <u>weak</u> and <u>vulnerable</u>.

[NOTE: The underlined words represent fill-ins from the student version.]

We all ask ourselves three central questions in life:

1. Who am I? It's about our <u>identity</u>.

2. Where do I belong? It's about our <u>security</u>.

3. What am I supposed to do? It's about our <u>significance</u>.

[NOTE: The underlined words represent fill-ins from the student version.]

Only God can provide authentic answers to those questions. Satan will attempt to deceive you into believing counterfeit things about yourself and seeking counterfeit solutions. This goes all the way back to the first book of the Bible and humanity's first sin.

Read Genesis 3:8-13 as a group:

"When the cool evening breezes were blowing, the man and his wife heard the Lord God walking about in the garden. So they hid from the Lord God among the trees. Then the Lord God called to the man, 'Where are you?'
He replied, 'I heard you walking in the garden, so I hid. I was afraid because I was naked.'
'Who told you that you were naked?' the Lord God asked. 'Have you eaten from the tree whose fruit I commanded you not to eat?'
The man replied, 'It was the woman you gave me who gave me the fruit, and I ate it.'
Then the Lord God asked the woman, "What have you done?'
'The serpent deceived me,' she replied. 'That's why I ate it.'"
Genesis 3:8-13 (NLT)

Three obstacles to getting the right answer:

1. We fear because of shame.
How can shame create fear?

2. We hide because of insecurity.
Why do our insecurities cause us to hide?

3. We blame because of denial.
Why do we blame other people or life's circumstances instead of taking responsibility?

Three ways to overcome these obstacles so we can answer the three big questions:

1. Know who you are

God wants you to think accurately of yourself. This kind of thinking will free you.

2. Connect with other Christians
You were designed as one piece to a much larger body — the body of Christ.

3. Use your talents and gifts to serve God and others
Get focused on how you can use your spiritual gifts to honor God and serve others.

live it out

[NOTE: Challenge your students to follow these application steps in the next week.]

1. Read 1 Corinthians 12:4-11 and Ephesians 4:11-16. These passages of Scripture also talk about the spiritual gifts God gives His followers.

2. Read days 21-25 of your daily devotional.

3. Do a self-assessment this week. Take a 3x5 card, and draw a line in the middle. On the top, write "My Top 3 Strengths" and on the bottom, write "My Top 3 Weaknesses." Talk to your parents and your friends about who you really are — with the goal of reaching an honest, sober self-assessment. Bring the card back next week so we can talk about it as a group.

[NOTE: Consider ending your small group with a time of prayer for each other, or you as the leader, may choose to be the only person praying aloud. Nudge your students out of their comfort zones when it comes to prayer — but don't push them off the deep end.]

Experiencing Authentic Community

Serving in love (Romans 12:9-13)

think about it

Nobody likes a fake. And plastic smiles don't last long when the heat gets turned up. True friends stand by our side during the best of times and the toughest of days. They don't abandon us, they don't walk away, and they don't reject us when they see our flaws.

We live in a culture that talks about BFFs, yet we see so many adults who lack deep, meaningful friendships with the people around them. Can you strive for something greater? Can you achieve solid relationships with others? Can you experience the kind of authentic community God desires for you? Yes, you can!

REVIEW

1. Last week's small group lesson focused on having a *sober* and honest evaluation of yourself as an r12 Christian. We talked about our search for identity, security, and significance, and how God offers the authentic answers — Satan only offers counterfeits. Your challenges at the end of the lesson included reading 1 Corinthians 12:4-11 and Ephesians 4:11-16, and doing a self-assessment with help from friends and family members.

[NOTE: Take time to review the self-assessments. If students brought back their 3x5 cards, great! If not, ask them to do their best to recall what friends and family members said were among their top strengths and top weaknesses. Ask your students if they were surprised by any of the answers, and if so, why.]

2. Your devotional readings this week focused on *serving* others in love. You read about being real and authentic, meeting people's needs, loving people the way Jesus loved people, seeking quality friendships with other Christians, and building authentic community.

get it started

Opening Question

How long can you really stay friends with a person who always seems fake? How does that "fakeness" hurt your friendship?

[NOTE: Bring some real flowers and some artificial flowers to your small group. If you have a group of girls, ask them how they'd feel if a boyfriend or significant guy friend gave a gift of artificial flowers. If you have a group of guys, ask them how they think a girl would feel if they gave a gift of artificial flowers. Then ask them the four questions we've included in the student version of this week's lesson.]

1. What message does a gift of artificial flowers communicate?

2. Maybe you can't afford a dozen roses, so what are some other good, healthy ways to express your love to people you care about deeply?

3. What's the connection between loving someone and displaying love through actions?

4. You probably don't want to give flowers — or receive flowers — from everyone at church, so what are some real-life ways to show that you love and care about other Christians?

talk it over

When the real <u>you</u> meets real <u>needs</u> for the right <u>reasons</u> in the right <u>way</u>, you have experienced <u>authentic</u> community.

[NOTE: The underlined words represent fill-ins from the student version.]

Read Romans 12:9-13 as a group:

"Don't just pretend to love others. Really love them. Hate what is wrong. Hold tightly to what is good. Love each other with genuine affection, and take delight in honoring each other. Never be lazy, but work hard and serve the Lord enthusiastically. Rejoice in our confident hope. Be patient in trouble, and keep on praying. When God's people are in need, be ready to help them. Always be eager to practice hospitality."
Romans 12:9-13 (NLT)

This passage focuses on your relationship with other Christians

Why do many Christians pretend to love other Christians?

How do you know if you genuinely love another person? How easy or difficult is it for you to genuinely love other people?
[NOTE: It can be tough to evaluate genuine love, but key indicators are consistency, demonstration through actions, faithfulness, availability during tough times, compassion, willingness to listen, and so on.]

Look at verse 11. Why does God care if we're lazy? How is it related to our spiritual maturity?
[NOTE: Being lazy is different from sleeping in on Saturday mornings. Being lazy is about lacking direction and not seeking God's purposes and plans for life. It dishonors God.]

How easily do you practice patience during difficult times? How can prayer help you in those situations?

Think about the last time you served or helped a person in need. How did it feel? How would your life be different if you were constantly on the lookout for those opportunities?

What are some ways you can practice hospitality to other Christians? How can you become a more generous r12 Christian?

Does God care about our motives as long as our actions are good? Explain your answer.
[NOTE: This can be a fun question for your group. God cares about our actions AND our motives. Good actions without right motives — well, that's how the Pharisees acted, and we know Jesus wasn't pleased with them!]

"Playing church" isn't much fun. It's all about religious rules and regulations. It becomes mundane and boring. And ultimately, it will kill you spiritually.

Read Acts 5:1-11 as a group:

"But there was a certain man named Ananias who, with his wife, Sapphira, sold some property. He brought part of the money to the apostles, claiming it was the full amount. With his wife's consent, he kept the rest.
Then Peter said, ' Ananias, why have you let Satan fill your heart? You lied to the Holy Spirit, and you kept some of the money for yourself. The property was yours to sell or not sell, as you wished. And after selling it, the money was also yours to give away. How could you do a thing like this? You weren't lying to us but to God!'
As soon as Ananias heard these words, he fell to the floor and died. Everyone who heard about it was terrified. Then some young men got up, wrapped him in a sheet, and took him out and buried him.
About three hours later his wife came in, not knowing what had happened. Peter asked her, 'Was this the price you and your husband received for your land?'
'Yes, she replied, 'that was the price.'
And Peter said, 'How could the two of you even think of conspiring to test the Spirit of the Lord like this? The young men who buried your husband are just outside the door, and they will carry you out, too.' Instantly, she fell to the floor and died. When the young men came in and saw that she was dead, they carried her out and buried her beside her husband. Great fear gripped the entire church and

everyone else who heard what had happened."
Acts 5:1-11 (NLT)

Why do you think God decided that the punishment for Ananias and Sapphira's lies would be death? What does that tell you about how much God values and rewards honesty?
[NOTE: The issue with Ananias and Sapphira wasn't that they didn't give God 100% of the profits from the sale of their land; it was that they LIED about it. Read Acts 4:36-37 for a comparison with someone who was honest.]

Read John 13:34-35 as a group:

"So now I am giving you a new commandment: Love each other. Just as I have loved you, you should love each other. Your love for one another will prove to the world that you are my disciples."
John 13:34-35 (NLT)

Why is Christians' love for each other such a powerful witness and testimony to the world?
[NOTE: Authentic love points people toward God and reveals the reality of God's love for each of us and for humanity.]

Pair up with another person in the group for this question:

Think about the Scripture passages we've discussed this week. What are some ways we can put these truths and instructions into practice in our youth group? How can you as teenagers lead the way in our church?

Come back together as a group to share answers to the previous question.

live it out

[NOTE: Challenge your students to follow these application steps in the next week.]

1. Read 1 Corinthians 13 every day.

2. Read days 26-30 of your daily devotional.

3. Look for a way this week to meet the needs of a friend or stranger. It can be a simple task, or it can be something you do every day for the next week. And if you want to take things to the next level, get together with some friends from your small group or youth ministry and volunteer in the community. Feed the homeless, clean up a community park, distribute coats and blankets

to the needy, help at a nearby school — find some way to reach out and serve in love.

[NOTE: Consider ending your small group with a time of prayer for each other, or you as the leader, may choose to be the only person praying aloud. Nudge your students out of their comfort zones when it comes to prayer — but don't push them off the deep end.]

Prayer

God, You're so much more powerful than I am, and nothing is impossible for You. Help me learn how to rely on you every day for answers and protection and transformation. I want to become a radical example of a changed life, but I know that only happens as I become more like You. Make me into a growing, healthy, authentic r12 Christian who is rooted in a deep relationship with You. Amen.

Overcoming the Evil Aimed at You

Supernaturally responding to evil with good (Romans 12:14-21)

think about it

Enemies don't deserve forgiveness or mercy or love. Enemies deserve revenge and payback and retribution. That's the way it works in our world. If you've been hurt, find the person who did it and strike back.

But as r12 Christians, we're called to make different choices. Of course, "different" doesn't always mean "easy." It's tough to forgive the people who've hurt, abandoned, betrayed, and gossiped about us. Yet God calls us to take that huge step and forgive. It's part of His call to supernaturally overcome evil with good.

REVIEW

1. Last week's small group lesson focused on *serving* others in love as r12 Christians. We talked about the importance of having a genuine, authentic love for other Christians and the impact this love can have on the world around us. Your challenges at the end of the lesson included reading 1 Corinthians 13 every day and meeting the needs of a stranger or friend — or working together with friends to meet a need in the community.

2. Your devotional readings this week focused on *supernaturally* responding to evil with good. You read about preparing for tough times in life, loving the people who hate you, praying for the people who've caused you pain, rejecting revenge and retaliation, and becoming a radical example of a changed life.

get it started

Opening Question

How many hours or minutes have you gone without sinning in your life? How often do you need to experience forgiveness?

Interactive Opening

[NOTE: This is an opportunity to make the idea of forgiveness personal and relevant. Talk with your students about a recent news event — ideally, something in your community — that involves someone who does not deserve forgiveness. Bring in a newspaper clip or show a recorded news segment talking about what happened. If you can't find a local example, choose a national or statewide news item — it's important to have a newspaper or media clip for this, because it will help students engage and learn on multiple levels. After discussing the news event, transition into the three questions we've included in the student version of this lesson.]

1. Are these some crimes or events that are beyond forgiveness? Is it possible some people have done something so bad that they don't deserve forgiveness? Explain your answer.

2. How do you typically respond when someone does something that hurts you? Do you immediately look for a way to retaliate, or do you withdraw? Why?

3. What do you think Jesus would say to the person we read about in this news event? How would He approach the situation?

talk it over

Read Romans 12:14-21 as a group:

"Bless those who persecute you. Don't curse them; pray that God will bless them. Be happy with those who are happy, and weep with those who weep. Live in harmony with each other. Don't be too proud to enjoy the company of ordinary people. And don't think you know it all! Never pay back evil with more evil. Do things in such a way that everyone can see you are honorable. Do all that you can to live in peace with everyone. Dear friends, never take revenge. Leave that to the righteous anger of God. For the Scriptures say, 'I will take revenge; I will pay them back,' says the Lord. Instead, 'If your enemies are hungry, feed them. If they are thirsty, give them something to drink. In doing this, you will heap burning coals of shame on their heads.' Don't let evil conquer you, but conquer evil by doing good." Romans 12:14-21 (NLT)

This passage focuses on your relationship with non-believers.

These are some pretty powerful verses — and may feel overwhelming to actually live out! What's your initial response to reading and hearing these words from the Apostle Paul?

Think of a recent time when you've forgiven another person — or when someone has forgiven you. What impact did this experience have on you?

What if you're dealing with a situation where YOU have caused an issue, even though you see the other person as an enemy? How should you handle this situation?

When do you find it easy to forgive? When do you find it difficult? What's the difference?

What would our world look like if everyone always took revenge on the people who caused hurt and pain? What do you think it would be like to live in a world where everyone acted that way?

In Romans 12, Paul offers three steps we as r12 Christians can walk through as we supernaturally respond to the people who have hurt us:

1. Choose to <u>forgive</u> them
Release your desire for payback and vengeance. Ask God for help as you take this step. You won't feel like forgiving the person; it's a decision you make. And as we talked about in this past week's devotional readings, it may take a long time to reach the second and third steps in this process.

2. Choose to <u>identify</u> with them
It's easy to weep, rejoice, mourn, and celebrate with our friends. But with our enemies? That's tough! But as you work through the process of forgiveness, you will find times when you realize your attitudes and emotions have changed. You no longer want revenge against this person; you want God to bless and save and redeem this person.

3. Consider opportunities to <u>associate</u> with them
Depending on the situation, this may or may not be possible. Sometimes we simply need to forgive and move forward with life. But other times, we have opportunities to live at peace with our former enemies because we've turned the situation over to God. We've decided to let Him handle whatever consequences are necessary.

[NOTE: The underlined words represent fill-ins from the student version.]

It's important to remember that Paul's words in this passage echo the same ideas Jesus taught people.

Read Matthew 5:43-48 as a group:

"You have heard the law that says, 'Love your neighbor' and hate your enemy. But I say, love your enemies! Pray for those who persecute you! In that way, you will be acting as true children of your Father in heaven. For he gives his sunlight to both the evil and the good, and he sends rain on the just and the unjust alike. If you love only those who love you, what reward is there for that? Even corrupt tax collectors do that much. If you are kind only to your friends, how are you different

from anyone else? Even pagans do that. But you are to be perfect, even as your Father in heaven is perfect."
Matthew 5:43-48 (NLT)

Look at verse 44. What kinds of prayers might you pray for people who persecute you? How would those prayers be different from the way you pray for your closest friends?

Verse 47 says Christians who are only kind to their friends really aren't different from people who don't claim to follow Christ. How does it make you feel to hear and read those words from Jesus?

If we try to do all of these things in our own energy — without seeking and relying on God's strength — what are some of the likely results, and why?
[NOTE: Ultimately, our efforts fail when done in our own strength. We might see results, change, and impact for a period of time, but the lasting effects need God's involvement.]

Jesus' instruction to love and pray for your enemies is one of the greatest statements He made — and He backed it up with action, asking God to forgive His enemies while He was hanging on the Cross.

Closing Activity
Think about someone who has caused you pain because of hurt, rejection, gossip, or some other unfair action. This person doesn't deserve forgiveness, but you believe God wants you to forgive this person as a decision that can help you grow spiritually and become an even more mature r12 Christian.

[NOTE: Give students a chance to practice forgiveness by writing down the names of people (or a person) who have caused hurt and pain. Give your students a couple of minutes to pray about this person. Be sensitive to the unique needs and situations of your students.]

live it out
[NOTE: Challenge your students to follow these application steps in the next week.]

1. Re-read Romans 12 and highlight or circle the words and phrases that have had the greatest impact on you during this small group series.

2. Look back at the prayer journal you started keeping in the first week of this small group series. What prayers has God answered? What are you continuing

to pray about each day? Give God thanks for the answers that have arrived — and the answers He will provide in the days and weeks ahead.

3. Journal about what it means to live a life that is totally surrendered to God. How will you continue to grow in this area, now that your small group has finished this series?

[NOTE: Consider ending your small group with a time of prayer for each other, or you as the leader may choose to be the only person praying aloud. Nudge your students out of their comfort zones when it comes to prayer — but don't push them off the deep end.]

Small Group Studies offered by Chip Ingram.

GOD: AS HE LONGS FOR YOU TO SEE HIM

How would you describe God? Awesome? All Powerful? Creator? While we cannot know Him exhaustively, we can know Him truly. And God longs for you to see Him as He truly is. Join Chip in this fascinating series studying the seven attributes of God.

MIRACLE OF LIFE CHANGE

Is life change really possible? If we're honest most of us would answer, "No." You've tried numerous programs that promise big changes, but in reality, deliver very little results. You long for transformation, but don't know where to begin. There's good news for you and there is hope. Life change is possible!

r12: LIVING ON THE EDGE

Being a genuine disciple of Christ flows out of a relationship with Him. It's about experiencing God's grace, not earning His love through performance. A real relationship with Jesus Christ will produce a follower whose life looks progressively more like His life. Romans 12 provides a relational profile of an authentic disciple: someone who is surrendered to God, separate from the world's values, sober in self-assessment, serving in love and supernaturally responding to evil with good. Christians who live out this kind of lifestyle are what we call r12 Christians.

INVISIBLE WAR

Beneath our tangible landscape lurks an invisible spiritual realm where an unseen battle rages. It's real and it's dangerous. If you're prepared to remove the blinders and gaze into the unseen world, Chip is ready to take you there.

EFFECTIVE PARENTING IN A DEFECTIVE WORLD

Raising children is a tough challenge in today's world. Peers and pop culture exert a never-ending pressure on kids. Many come from split homes. But the good news is that God has been working with people from bad situations for a long time! In Effective Parenting you will learn how God's principles for raising children still work today. Packed with practical advice, this series will give struggling parents a vision for their children's future and life-changing help for today!

EXPERIENCING GOD'S DREAM FOR YOUR MARRIAGE

Would you like a fresh breeze to blow in your marriage? Do you long for a marriage where intimacy and communication are a reality instead of a dream? "Experiencing God's Dream for Your Marriage" is a topical series by Chip Ingram examining God's design for marriage, with practical instruction to help you make your marriage what God desires it to be.

FIVE LIES THAT RUIN RELATIONSHIPS

Have you ever looked back over a situation or relationship in your life and wondered how it became so messy or difficult? In Five Lies that Ruin Relationships, we'll define five of the most common lies that have the potential to ruin relationships with those we love. What we think about life determines how we live it, so there is power in knowing and applying God's truth when confronted with lies and discovering the freedom He longs for us to enjoy in our relationships.

LOVE, SEX & LASTING RELATIONSHIPS

Everyone wants to love and be loved. The pursuit of "true love" is everywhere you look! It's romanticized on TV and in the movies we watch. There are books about it, songs about it, internet dating, and even seminars on it... all of which are designed to "help" you find that special someone to love. So why is "true love" so elusive? Could it be that the picture of love we see in today's culture is nothing more than an illusion? If so, what does real love look like? In this series, you'll discover that there is a better way to find love, stay in love, and grow in intimacy for a lifetime. Chip Ingram delivers to us God's prescription for building relationships that last a lifetime.

TRUE SPIRITUALITY ACCORDING TO JESUS (r12)

True Spirituality According to Jesus is a small group study that complements the Living on the Edge book. The book looks specifically at Romans, chapter 12 and the small group study looks at what Jesus said and modeled for us about the principles in Romans 12. Taken together, this is a dynamic study that will encourage you to become an r12 Christian. Romans 12 is the START HERE for the Christian life. What most Christians sadly misunderstand is that God isn't into religious activities or performance-based Christianity. Instead, Romans 12 reveals to us a relational profile of what it means to be a disciple, as well as a proven pathway to becoming more like Jesus every day.